HIDDEN C

The slavery business and North East England
1600-1865

John Charlton

Tyne Bridge Publishing

*Africa and the Atlantic Ocean
published in 1714 in John Nutt's 'Atlas Geographicus'.*

For Anna, Mick, Beck, Siobhan, Mark and Davey

Acknowledgements

Tyne Bridge Publishing and Newcastle Libraries gratefully acknowledge the invaluable assistance of the following partners in the Remembering Slavery Project, who accomplished all the groundwork: Tyne and Wear Museums, Northumberland Collections Service, Newcastle Literary and Philosophical Society, Tyne and Wear Archives Service, University of Newcastle Robinson Library Special Collections.

Tyne Bridge Publishing would like to extend thanks to the British Museum, the National Portrait Gallery, and to the Suffolk (Ipswich) Record Office for their kind assistance. Hazel Edwards and Tamsin Lilley of Tyne and Wear Museums have given constant support. Anne Waller of Newcastle Libraries has been most helpful.

We also thank Professor James Walvin for his generous advice, and for writing the foreword.

The author's detailed acknowledgements appear on page 174.

Hidden Chains is part of the Remembering Slavery 2007 Archive and Mapping Research Project led by Newcastle's Literary and Philosophical Society. It is published in association with Tyne and Wear Museums.

The occasional black and white engravings are reproduced from Thomas Hugo's, *Bewick's Woodcuts* (1870) unless otherwise indicated. The illustration of the *Brooks* on the front cover is from Tyne and Wear Archives (DX449/1).

ISBN: 9781857951233

Published by
City of Newcastle upon Tyne
Newcastle Libraries & Information Service
Tyne Bridge Publishing
2008

This publication has been made possible with funding from the Heritage Lottery Fund, the Department for Culture Media and Sport, Renaissance North East, the Museums, Libraries and Archives Council, the Northern Rock Foundation and Tyne and Wear Museums' Business Partners.

Printed by Elanders Hindson, North Tyneside

Contents

Look to the far left of this painting and you will see a small black page boy. This painting by Thomas Bardwell shows Captain Robert Fenwick and family at Norham Castle and was painted around 1740.

Foreword by James Walvin

Few scholars today would dispute the impact of the Atlantic slave system on the development and nature of British life in the 17th and 18th centuries. Indeed the more we learn about slavery, the more important it becomes. Here was a major economic and social phenomenon which saw the enforced movement of millions of Africans into the Americas, and all for the development and material well-being of colonial and metropolitan societies. Though the British did not initiate the process, they brought it to new peaks of efficiency and profitability. Yet the most curious aspect remains: why should the British turn against the slave trade, and slavery itself, when much of the evidence suggests it remained a profitable system?

This historical conundrum has taxed historians for years, and the debate rumbles on. There has been a flood of recent scholarship, on the slave trade, on plantation economies, on the industrial and financial underpinning (and consequences) of slavery – and on the complex political process which saw slavery destroyed. In this welter of scholarship it is sometimes difficult to make sense of the whole – to see Atlantic slavery in the round.

For too long British historians have tended to think of Africans and their contribution to the rise of the modern Atlantic as a distant topic; something that evolved on the far side of the Atlantic. Slavery itself has long remained out of sight and out of mind – an area of specialism for historians of Africa or the Americas.

Yet it was British capital, British ships and sailors, British ports and British-backed plantations that enabled those same Africans to tap the wealth of the Americas. And much of that slave-grown produce (sugar and tobacco for instance) returned to Britain for consumption, for processing and for re-shipping to other parts of the world. Oddly, there have been reminders of the importance of slavery to Britain staring historians in the face; black faces in the 18th century crowd, the sweetening of the national diet, tobacco smoke in the nation's coffee shops, sugar bowls in costly tea-services. But such superficial evidence needs to be challenged and explained.

What has been required is more systematic research into these and other manifestations of slavery.

Scholars have, in recent years, provided some stunning data on the size and significance of the slave trade itself. Similarly, we now know a great deal about the lives of Africans in the America and of their persistent resistance to their captivity. The bi-centenary of the abolition of the British slave trade in 1807, commemorated around the Atlantic in 2007, provided an opportunity to think more broadly, and more critically, about the slave trade and slavery. Indeed it is hard to think of a comparable historical commemoration which spawned so many, diverse and popular commemorations in recent British experience. Inevitably, 1807/2007 proved more problematic than many people imagined. The initial reaction (that here was a chance to celebrate the British at their best) soon gave way to a more critical and contrary view. After all, though Parliament passed the abolition Act in 1807, it had passed dozens of pro-slave trade Acts in the century before. Equally, it had to be stressed that the slave trade continued after 1807 and that slavery itself was not abolished until many years later.

Still, 2007 offered many people the chance to re-think a critical moment in British (and British global) experience. And as local groups pondered how best to commemorate abolition, it became clear that they needed to say something distinctive – something local perhaps – about slavery and abolition. There was, after all, little point in merely repeating the general story of abolition. The result was that institutions (libraries, galleries, museums, archives, local authorities) sought to address abolition from a local and regional perspective. What emerged was a quite remarkable national mosaic: local exhibitions and commemorations that were distinct from each other but which, when placed together, came together to form a national picture that had a great variety of local distinctions.

It is easy to see why slavery and the slave trade were woven into the history of London and of western England. We know of the major importance of London, of Bristol and Liverpool, and their regional hinterlands, in shaping and benefiting from the slave trade. But eastern England has always seemed geographically distant from, and relatively unaffected by, Atlantic history. The importance of John Charlton's new book is that it confounds this old impression by giving old arguments and theories a new, regional interpretation. Migrations to and from the

Americas, the return of capital and investment to the North East, trade and business links, maritime and commercial connections, the impact of slave grown produce – all these and more form the substance of this refreshing reappraisal. Newcastle was clearly never likely to be as important as ports in western England – yet that port, and the huge hinterland it served, was enmeshed in the world of Atlantic slavery like all other corners of the kingdom. John Charlton's account is pioneering and revealing: a bold statement of new findings and a call for further investigation into the links between regional North East England and the world of Atlantic slavery.

James Walvin
Professor Emeritus, University of York

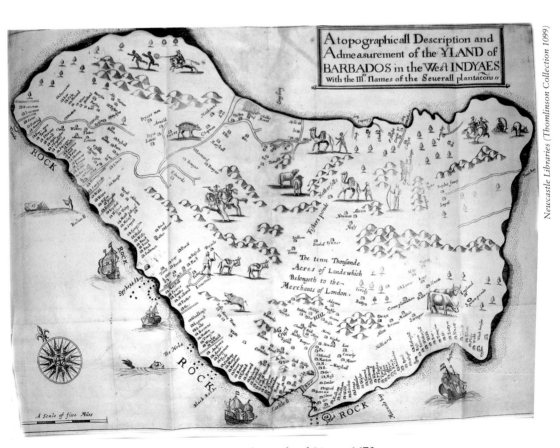

From 'A History of the Barbadoes' by Richard Ligon, 1673.

Newcastle Libraries (Thomlinson Collection 1099)

Barrels of sugar leaving Antigua in the Caribbean.

Some North East plantation owners employed managers to look after their Caribbean estates. These slaves are digging cane holes.

Introduction: Slavery and the Atlantic

The Atlantic slave trade was built upon a shocking system. Buying human beings who had been chased, captured and wrenched from their families and villages, imprisoning them in shackles below decks and subjecting them to appalling violence for months on the Atlantic crossing must rate as one of the greatest crimes in history. Selling these uprooted people like cattle in slave markets in Barbados, Jamaica and Charleston added a second act to the ghastly drama. The final act was carting them off to lifetimes of unremitting toil, usually shortened by overwork, disease or beatings. The business made money in vast quantities for ship captains, slave traders, planters, merchants and absentee gentlemen owners in England.

The Atlantic slave trade has its origins early in the 16th century, mainly perpetrated at that time by the Spanish and Portuguese. English freebooters, such as John Hawkins and Francis Drake, had participated as traders in Elizabethan times but it was in the early 17th century that a comprehensive English business developed with trading posts in West Africa, a plantation complex in North America and the Caribbean and merchant houses in London, Bristol and Liverpool. The English slave trade continued to the beginning of the 19th century and slavery, in the British Empire, until 1833.

Many thousands of British men, and rather fewer women, made the journey west as traders, planters, farmers, soldiers and sailors. Many settled. In Britain great businesses were created from the colonial product. Enormous wealth was accumulated for further investment and often conspicuous consumption. It would be difficult to overestimate the importance of this wealth to the development of Britain as a leading world power. It is also all too easy to underestimate the degree to which the slavery business reached every corner of the British Isles geographically, economically and socially.

In 2007 the bi-centenary of the legal ending of the slave trade in the British Empire was celebrated. Large exhibitions were held in Bristol, Liverpool, Glasgow and London, the first three long-known as cities built

Around 12 million Africans were taken from the West African coast to the islands of the Caribbean and to North and South America. This map of the Slave Coast and its forts was published in 1714 in John Nutt's 'Atlas Geographicus'.

on the labour of slaves. London, as the capital and the political and business hub of the Empire, was right at the centre of a global web.

North East England has been celebrated as a pioneer of industrialisation, but very little attention has been paid to its connections with slavery and the New World. Yet Newcastle was one of the most important towns and seaports in the age of colonial slavery. It was no Bristol or Liverpool, and the Atlantic and Caribbean were not the main focus of its sea-borne business activity, but the focus on coal and the London and Baltic sea trades has meant that the North East's connections to Atlantic and African activity have remained largely invisible.

Very few specialised ships were built and equipped on North East rivers for the Guinea trade. Collier brigs returning from the West Indies with cargoes of sugar and rum apparently revealed no sign of involvement on the 'middle passage' of the trade from Africa across the Atlantic. Unlike Bristol merchants, whose servants were often black people bought directly from slave ships, Newcastle merchants employed mainly north country girls and boys. Members of elite circles would have known that the occasional black person worked in North East country houses, but black servants were not omnipresent, as they were in Bristol. There were a few advertisements in the Newcastle press for information about absconding black servants, but they were evidently not pursued with 'hue and cry' and there were no dramatic public arrests that we know of. Much more common were advertisements and rewards for runaway bonded pitmen and bound apprentices.

There is also relative silence in the histories of the North East about the campaigns for abolition of the slave trade and slavery. The Unitarian minister William Turner's part in abolitionist activity has been noted[1] but histories of early radical politics in the region have given the issue little importance.

The invisibility of the region's slavery connection may have contributed to the apparent lack of social tension when demands for abolition were raised in the late 18th century. Tyneside, for example, was a small community, both socially and in physical size, and businessmen with slave trade connections lived and worked alongside keen abolitionists, with no apparent antagonism.

It should be noted that the account offered here is provisional. Right up to press new material has been turned up, some of which it has been impossible to incorporate at this stage. It is likely that the story will be much revised in future.

Facts and figures

Crossing the Atlantic journey times
In the 17th century the North Atlantic crossing could take between 45 and 138 days at sea.
In the 18th century the crossing was reduced to 42-85 days.
The Middle Passage from Africa to the Caribbean would last between 40 and 70 days.

Comparative value
£100 in 1830 is equivalent to approximately £6000 in 2008.
£25,000 in 1836 is equivalent to approximately £2.5 million in 2008.

(Lawrence H. Officer & Samuel H. Williamson, *Measures of Worth, 2007*; www.MeasuringWorth.com)

The main players: slavery and abolition

National leaders in the movement for abolition

Thomas Fowell Buxton, MP.

Thomas Clarkson, leading propagandist and organiser.

Charles Grey (Earl Grey), Prime Minister.

Henry Grey, Viscount Howick, strongly anti-slavery

William Knibb, Baptist Missionary.

Sir Ralph Milbanke, MP for Durham.

James Stephen senior and junior, writers, campaigners
and organisers.

George Stephen, son and brother of the above,
organiser of the Agency Committee.

Joseph Sturge, MP, speaker, writer, campaigner.

George Thompson, speaker, writer and organiser.

William Wilberforce, MP.

Earl Grey

Local/national abolitionists

Jonathan Backhouse, Quaker banker.

Joseph Cowen, MP, campaigner, newspaper proprietor.

John Fenwick, Baptist and Newcastle lawyer.

Edward Pease, MP, Quaker.

Elizabeth (Pease) Nichol, Quaker campaigner.

James Field Stanfield, seaman and actor.

Henry Taylor, Quaker seaman from North Shields.

Dr Thomas Trotter, sailed on the slave ship *Brooks*.

William Turner, Unitarian Minister.

Dr Thomas Winterbottom, served as a medical officer
in Sierra Leone.

William Woodman, Morpeth campaigner.

Thomas Clarkson

Elizabeth Pease

Supporting abolition though not necessarily active

William Ord MP.

Matthew White Ridley I MP.

Matthew White Ridley II MP.

M.W. Ridley

North Easterners involved in the slavery business

Ward Cadogan, owner of the Pickerings Plantation in Barbados, and Brinkburn.

John Erasmus Blackett, major Newcastle merchant gentleman, father-in-law of Stead.

Mary Barrett (née Graham Clarke), mother of Elizabeth Barrett-Browning, poet.

James Graham Clarke, son of John below, Newcastle businessman.

J. Graham Clarke

John Graham Clarke, Newcastle West India merchant, banker, owner of glass works and coal mine.

John Altham Graham Clarke, son of the above, married Jamaican planter's daughter.

John Hussey Delaval, owner of East Florida plantation.

Robert Hutton, seaman and trader with Africa.

Joseph Lamb, coal merchant and Mayor of Newcastle.

William Richardson, South Shields mariner.

Sir John Trevelyan, 4th Baronet, of Wallington, plantation owner in Grenada.

Sir John Trevelyan, 5th Baronet.

J.E. Blackett

North Americans with North East connections

Edward Cook, Alnwick farmer's son – Baltimore.

Johnson family from Kibblesworth – Carolina .

Charles Cotesworth Pinckney, planter, politician.

Benjamin Stead, Northumberland gentleman – Carolina.

American visitors

William Wells Brown, former slave.

Henry Highland Garnett, former slave and organiser.

William Lloyd Garrison, American abolitionist.

Frederick Douglass, former slave, speaker, writer and organiser.

F. Douglass

DECLARATION

OF THE OBJECTS OF

THE NEWCASTLE UPON TYNE SOCIETY

FOR PROMOTING THE

Gradual Abolition of Slavery

THROUGHOUT THE BRITISH DOMINIONS.

NEWCASTLE UPON TYNE:

PRINTED BY W. A. MITCHELL, ST. NICHOLAS' CHURCH-YARD.

1823.

I

The fight against the dirty business

The North East of England proved to be one of the strongest areas in the struggle against the slave trade and subsequently the institution of slavery itself.

Newcastle around 1829.

Newcastle Libraries (local colour prints)

Newcastle's new Assembly Rooms, Westgate, around 1789.

1 The profligacy of this age

Economic change in the 18th century brought prosperity to the gentry and a growing urban middle class. Their conspicuous consumption sparked controversy contributing to the birth of a radical political culture in the North East of England, especially in Newcastle, its regional capital. The presence of several strands of dissenting religion was an important seed bed for this development. Anti-slavery sentiment was cultivated in this rich environment.

A group of wealthy patrons hired the eminent architect William Newton to design the Assembly Rooms in Westgate, Newcastle, which opened in 1776. The burgeoning self confidence of this coterie is well expressed in this inscription to be found on a brass plaque on the building:

> *In an age*
> *When the polite arts,*
> *By general Encouragement and Emulation,*
> *Have advanced to a State of Perfection*
> *Unknown in any former Period*
> *The first Stone of this edifice*
> *Dedicated to the most elegant Recreation,*
> *Was laid by William Lowes Esq.,*
> *On the 16th day of May, 1774*

A concert programme indicates that patrons could pay up to three shillings and sixpence per ticket at a time when a pitman's earnings might average 18 shillings per week, a keelman's 17 shillings and a seaman's 8 shillings. The gentry and growing middle class were private consumers of a vast array of goods: elegant furniture, delicate china, beautiful wall papers and draperies, musical instruments, bespoke clothing, perfumes, snuff boxes, elaborate jewellery, oil paintings, tobacco, cocoa, tea, coffee and mountains of sugar, and many of these items

Tyne and Wear Museums

Sugar sifter, 1778.

had their origins in the colonies. The North East economy dovetailed with a global economy in which slavery played a fundamental part.

Reverend James Murray was the minister of a dissenting chapel in High Bridge, Newcastle.[2] He was an abrasive and determined assailant of privilege and a great selector of biblical texts for his sermons, which were often thinly disguised attacks on hierarchy and were advertised in the weekly *Newcastle Chronicle*. The Tyne Bridge had been washed away in floods in 1772 and the Common Council was dragging its feet in rebuilding it, so his response to the opening of the Assembly Rooms was a sardonic verse:

> *When a stagnation*
> *Of trade, and the high price of provisions,*
> *Has reduced the poor to the greatest extremity:*
> *When the bridge, once over Tyne,*
> *At Newcastle, remained*
> *Entomb'd in the depths of the river,*
> *A heap of ruins,*
> *A chaos of disorder;*
> *To their everlasting disgrace, the gentlemen of Newcastle*
> *Continue to waste their time,*
> *And spend their substance,*
> *In celebrating the rites of Venus, and the ceremonies of Bacchus.*
> *Five thousand*
> *Pounds were raised by subscription,*
> *Through a vicious emulation to excel in politeness;*
> *And land, devoted to pious purposes,*
> *Was sold by the Vicar, a thing*
> *Unknown in any former period;*
> *And this fabric*
> *Was raised*
> *On the ruins of religion, and the morals of mankind.*
> *The pious sanction of William L——s, Esq.,*
> *Engraved on brass, continues to show the profligacy of this age.*

Dissent was becoming highly politicised.

During the late 1760s and early 1770s the London radical, John Wilkes,[3] enjoyed the support of many Newcastle people in his efforts to get elected to parliament. The same people railed against property developers' attempts to encroach on the Town Moor and organised a pro-American petition to Parliament on its conduct of the War of Independence that began in 1776. 'No taxation without representation' was a powerful sentiment in Newcastle as well as in North America.

For much of his life Thomas Bewick[4] was involved in Newcastle discussion clubs – groups of artisans and small employers who met to hear the news and exchange opinions. It seems quite likely that they were also the organising focus for those involved in radical campaigns during the 1770s and that membership overlapped with religious dissenters in the campaigns for the abolition of the slave trade.

Thomas Bewick

Natural History Society of Northumberland

Jeremiah Spence was a Scots immigrant to Newcastle, and James Murray was his pastor. In November 1775, Spence's son, Thomas, gave a lecture to the first, short-lived, Philosophical Society, and it appeared as a pamphlet called *Property in Land: Every One's Right*. Calling for common ownership of the land, it was a frontal attack on property rights. Bewick's Memoirs record that Spence caused considerable controversy even among dissenting circles. Vigorous and often heated debate was rife. The town's printers were kept busy by angry pamphleteers.[5]

Newcastle Libraries

Quakers and Unitarians had had an unbroken presence in Newcastle from the late 17th century despite considerable persecution. Some Quaker mannerisms tended to isolate them socially, but they were respected for their business acumen and probity. By the 18th century Newcastle had a substantial

The Wesleyan Orphan House on Newcastle's Northumberland Street.

Mansion House, City of Newcastle

John Wesley preaches at Newcastle. He thundered against slavery.

dissenting community, though schisms were very common, especially among Presbyterians. They were not politically radical, except in the broadest anti-authoritarian sense, but they had come into existence out of opposition to the hierarchies of the established Presbyterian and Episcopalian churches in Scotland and the Anglican Church south of the border. It is likely that their greatest support in Newcastle was among the keelmen and shipwrights in the east end, many of whom were of Scots origin. Most dissenting chapels were in their part of town.

John Wesley and his brother, Charles, visited the American colonies in the 1730s and John formed very strong views on slavery which he was not shy to publicise. In 1742 he preached in Newcastle to large open air audiences and he strongly appealed to poorer and middling folks. The town became 'the northern corner stone' of Methodism and the first chapel, seating 500 people, was opened in Northumberland Street before 1780. Wesley's pamphlet, *Thoughts on Slavery*, was published in 1774[6] and attacked seamen involved in the slave trade. In it, he thundered:

> Are you a man? Then you should have an human heart. But have you indeed? What is your heart made of? Is there no such principle as Compassion there? Do you never feel another's pain? Have you no Sympathy? No sense of human woe? No pity for the miserable? When you saw the flowing eyes, the heaving

breasts, or the bleeding sides and tortured limbs of your fellow-creatures, was you a stone, or a brute? Did you look upon them with the eyes of a tiger? When you squeezed the agonizing creatures down in the ship, or when you threw their poor mangled remains into the sea, had you no relenting? Did not one tear drop from your eye, one sigh escape from your breast? Do you feel no relenting now? If you do not, you must go on, till the measure of your iniquities is full. Then will the Great GOD deal with You, as you have dealt with them, and require all their blood at your hands.[7]

Newcastle's sizeable Methodist community would have been well aware of Wesley's position. He preached in Newcastle four times between 1787 and his death in 1792, at the height of the first major abolitionist agitation.[8]

The national campaign against the slave trade emerged in the mid-1780s. By this time the Newcastle area had a seasoned radical public open to seeing the slavery business as an abomination requiring urgent action.

Newcastle Libraries (local colour prints)

An expression of Newcastle's prosperity: the Assembly Rooms and Westgate Road, looking towards St Nicholas' church, around 1789.

2   A plain statement of facts

*The first phase of anti-slavery agitation took fire in the late 1780s.
Attracting people in thousands, it flourished for only five years or so. A
product of the same critical sentiment that produced the French Revolution,
it floundered on the rapid growth of a conservative backlash after war
broke out between the British and the French in 1793*

In its early years the abolitionist movement was restricted mainly to elite
intellectual circles. Its leaders tended to live in or around London, close to
Parliament, where the main lobbying took place and where changes in
national policy could be enacted. They carried out research in Bristol and
Liverpool, the major slave trading ports, and it was there that Thomas
Clarkson learned the details of the slave trade: the routes, the ships and the
seamen. Armed with this extraordinarily detailed information, 'the plain
facts' he embarked on arduous tours of Britain.

In 1787 Clarkson's London Abolition Committee broadened the
campaign. The later 1780s were a time of ferment in Britain and elsewhere
(especially France), and the campaign for the improvement of the condition
and status of slaves fitted well with calls for reform of Parliament, an end to
government corruption and the removal of restrictions on religious
dissenters. It followed recent political divisions over the American War of
Independence. Clarkson wrote a report that summarised the horrors of the
slave trade and in January 1788, when his Committee was only a few
months old, they sent a copy to the Mayor of every English corporation,
inviting them to petition Parliament.[9]

Restrictions on religious dissenters and the American War of
Independence had raised strong feelings in Newcastle and were not merely
the concerns of a handful of zealous gentlemen. Moreover, the anti-slavery
issue had gone beyond the usual suspects and its broad humanitarian appeal
encompassed many mainstream Anglicans and political conservatives.

On February 12 Newcastle Common Council carried the following
resolution:

It is resolved and ordered that Mr. Recorder be requested to draw a petition from the Mayor Alderman Sheriff and the rest of the Common Council of this corporation to the Honourable The House of Commons, praying the said house to take into serious consideration the hardships which many of the natives of Africa suffer by means of the trade carried on for purchasing slaves to cultivate the lands in the West Indies, and to make such regulations therein, tending to the honour and interest of Great Britain, as to the wisdom and humanity of the house shall seem meet and it is further ordered that a Common Council be held on Saturday next to seal the said petition in case the same be then approved of.

Thomas Clarkson by Carl Frederick von Breda, 1788.

They met a week later and 'produced read and approved of' the petition, 'ordered that the same be engrossed and sealed under the common seal of this corporation and forwarded to London by John Eras[mus]. Blackett Esq.[10]

The Common Council was a conservative body of merchants and included two sugar importers, yet it was one of the first such bodies in Britain to take such a decision. Its decision may have reflected strong abolitionist sentiment in the town's guilds.

Parliamentary candidates for Newcastle were always very solicitous in their attention to the guilds (powerful organisations that combined the functions of business management and trades unionism), some of whose members formed the town's most radical constituency and showed heavy support for the Americans in the War of Independence. Some Newcastle men formed one of the Corresponding Societies that had grown up after the French Revolution of 1789, but we know little about it. In 1791 Thomas

Paine's *Rights of Man* was widely celebrated in the North East and a hostile report claimed that every pitman carried it in his back pocket. However, after the flight of King Louis XVI from Versailles in 1791, the ruling Jacobins proclaimed that they would export revolution. Only the doughtiest British republicans could openly support them, and the campaigns for relief for Roman Catholics and dissenters, and for parliamentary reform, were almost completely silenced, but the anti-slavery campaign persisted.

Newcastle Literary and Philosophical Society

William Turner, founder of Newcastle's Literary and Philosophical Society, in 1793.

William Turner was born in Wakefield in 1760. In 1781, aged 21, he was appointed as minister of the Hanover Square Unitarian Chapel in Newcastle, and was to stay there for 50 years. Unitarians represented the greatest challenge to received religious ideas by denying the Trinity of the Father, Son and Holy Ghost, but their interest in scientific and philosophical enquiry made them attractive to innovators in an era of rapid economic and technical change. Turner's first obituary said that 'the bent of his mind was altogether to the practical and tangible, rather than to the speculative or mysterious.' He founded the Literary and Philosophical Society in 1793, the New Institution in 1802, the Society of Antiquaries in 1813, the Mechanics Institute in 1824, the Natural History Society in 1829, a library and two schools. He was a polymath and an organiser.[11]

Clarkson was keen to tap into the broader radical constituency beyond Parliament and came to Newcastle in 1791. He may have explained the

London Abolition Committee's strategy, but Turner took responsibility for its execution. Abolition of slavery was at the heart of the faith of both Quakers and Unitarians, and though their numbers were small in Newcastle, Turner was able to organise a group of abolitionists. William Batson and Edward Prowitt were Unitarians from Turner's Hanover Square congregation. Hadwen Bragg, Anthony Clapham, Robert Ormston, and George Richardson were Quakers, as was Henry Taylor, a seaman from North Shields. Thomas Allason was the Anglican vicar of Heddon on the Wall. Methodists and Presbyterians were also involved, like the Reverend Smith of the Sallyport dissenting meeting house. They were mainly men of modest property, though Batson was a prosperous corn merchant. The first Newcastle anti-slavery society was founded in October. At least five of the committee of ten were Quakers who had nearly a decade of abolitionist activity behind them. They sent letters across the region inviting others to participate in a petition and called on the Aldermen and Common Council to allow the use of Newcastle Guildhall as a base for would-be signatories. At their second meeting in December they decided not to rush to a petition, but to print, publish and distribute 2,000 copies of Clarkson's *Abstract of Evidence against the slave trade*, since 'nothing more will be necessary but a plain statement of Facts, by Persons who speak, not from Hearsay, but from actual knowledge; and were subject to be cross examined by those who were interested to detect Misrepresentations.' Thomas Bewick was an abolitionist and his engraved medallion was used to decorate the frontispiece.

In January 1792 the *Newcastle Courant* published a letter by one, 'Humanus':

> Happening lately to be sometime from home the females in my family had in my absence perused a pamphlet entitled 'An address to the People of Great Britain on the Utility of refraining from the use of West India Sugar and Rum'. On my return, I was surprised to find that they had entirely left off the use of sugar, and banished it from the tea table. They were induced so to do, not on account of the present exorbitant price of that article, but from a persuasion that the consumer of an article procured by a horrid traffic, and the most inhuman treatment of their fellow creatures, is in some degree accessory to the crimes attending that pamphlet, which cannot be too often laid before the public as the pamphlet truly states, either to reprobate or

approve the measure; for West Indian Slavery must depend on their support for its existence, and it is in the power of every individual, to increase or lessen its extent.

The writer concluded that,

those numerous displays of humanity, of which this kingdom boasts, can scarce be supposed to have their foundations in any virtuous or valuable principle, if we continue to contribute in any degree to the encouragement of that traffic, which is founded in such injustice and cruelty as ought not to be heard of in an enlightened age, and which produces the utmost extent of misery, pain, labour and hunger, which human nature can endure, without terminating its existence.

The North East was an important centre of Quakerism and Unitarianism, and women in the congregation were able and ready to use their voices in the public sphere.

That month the Newcastle committee sent a copy of Clarkson's *Abstract* to the Master and Brethren of Newcastle Trinity House, the Stewards of the incorporated guilds in Newcastle and Gateshead, the ministers of every Parish Church and dissenting congregation and the Clerks of the Societies of Methodists and the Quakers, local sheriffs and JPs, and the mayors and aldermen of Newcastle, Durham and Berwick on Tweed corporations. Targeting official bodies and those in authority

Tyne and Wear Museums

Sugar-loaf nippers, 1750-1850, for cutting small pieces from a sugar loaf.

Tyne and Wear Museums

A silver coffee pot made by John Langlands, Newcastle upon Tyne, 1782.

Tyne and Wear Archives DX112/1

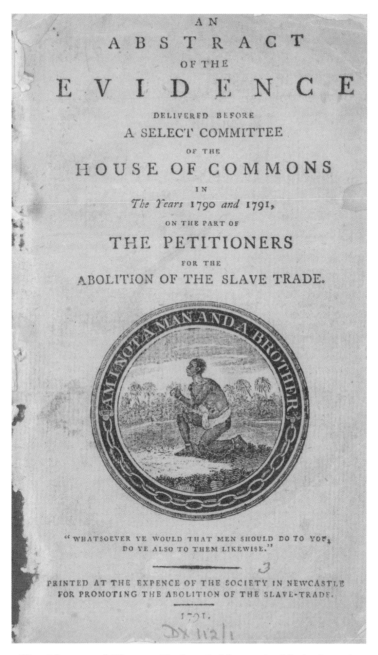

AN

ABSTRACT

OF THE

EVIDENCE

DELIVERED BEFORE

A SELECT COMMITTEE

OF THE

HOUSE OF COMMONS

IN

The Years 1790 *and* 1791,

ON THE PART OF

THE PETITIONERS

FOR THE

ABOLITION OF THE SLAVE TRADE.

"WHATSOEVER YE WOULD THAT MEN SHOULD DO TO YOU, DO YE ALSO TO THEM LIKEWISE."

PRINTED AT THE EXPENCE OF THE SOCIETY IN NEWCASTLE FOR PROMOTING THE ABOLITION OF THE SLAVE-TRADE.

1791.

The title page of Thomas Clarkson's 'Abstract' with the haunting image of the 'supplicant slave'. See page 53 for more about this image.

was probably intended to give the petition a semi-official status. They hoped that a more thorough knowledge of the subject would 'produce a general disposition to join in a respectful Petition to Parliament, for the entire abolition of this inhuman traffic.' It was a great success and people who might otherwise have seen it as the work of radicals became inveterate petitioners. The Stewards of the Newcastle guilds asked the Mayor to make facilities available for petitioners at the Guildhall, and he agreed.

There were six bookshops in the town where people could sign. Apparently women were not invited to sign, though a few may have done so. Leaving out juveniles and the very old, this left perhaps 12-15,000 possible Newcastle signatories and perhaps a further 5,000 from Gateshead. In the event, over 3,000 people signed, or about a third more than the number of those eligible to vote in parliamentary elections. (Per head of population perhaps only Manchester and Edinburgh exceeded Newcastle's signatories.) Sadly, the petition was burned in the great fire at the Houses of Parliament in 1834, so we can only guess at the signatories' social and religious composition, but craftsmen represented the majority of the literate population and were also the largest group to express an interest in political issues. Signing facilities were set up in Berwick, Morpeth, North and South Shields, Sunderland, Durham and Stockton on Tees, but also in Belford and Wooler which had 400 signatories each, and in Alnwick where there were 600, so the total number of signatories around the region would surely have exceeded that of Newcastle.[12]

Between 1791 and 1795 there were slave revolts on Jamaica, Grenada and St Domingue (Haiti). During the Fédon Rebellion in Grenada, Ninian Home, the planter-Governor, whose home was Paxton House just east of Berwick, lost his life. The rebellion in St Domingue was triggered by the French Revolution and affected the course of the abolition

Sir H.H. Johnson, 'The Negro in the New World', 1910

Toussaint L'Ouverture, the Haitian revolutionary leader, about 1795.

movement in Britain. There was satisfaction in seeing the French getting a bloody nose, but when the rebels held on and the revolt seemed to be successful, attitudes changed. A rebellion in one colony could have repercussions in others, including British possessions.

Newcastle Literary and Philosophical Society came into being just when open radical organisation became impossible. Its initial meetings took place in the spring and summer of 1793, weeks after Louis XVI was executed and the French declared war on Britain. The Society's major supporters included some people from the groups associated with reforming politics in the 1780s, but leading conservative establishment figures like the merchant and sometime Mayor, William Cramlington, participated. William Turner based the Society's rules on those of the Manchester Literary and Philosophical Society, though his Regulation VIII expressly forbade the consideration of 'all Politics of the day', because of the need to legitimise the Society at a very excitable and critical time. The Society was formally founded without incident and gave Newcastle's progressives a focus for organised intellectual life in the bleak decades of war and shortage.[13]

In 1792 over 500 petitions, with over 400,000 signatures, were submitted to Parliament. It was clear that a tremendous popular upsurge was beginning, but MPs failed to support motions in favour of abolition. Britain was soon to be at war with France and would become engulfed in patriotic fervour. Government and unofficial spies reported to the Home Secretary on 'suspicious' activities and political dissent of every kind was hounded from the streets and meeting places. Tom Paine[14] was burned in effigy at least 19 times on Tyneside.[15] William Wilberforce, the evangelical cleric and MP,[16] tried to maintain pressure for abolition in Parliament by attacking other reforms, but he was absurdly accused of Jacobinism. Campaigns for abolition outside Parliament were grouped with other reforming issues and were linked to revolutionary 'French ideas'. Clarkson became ill, possibly from depression, and disappeared from the movement for almost a decade.

Across the country, the anti-slave trade committees were disbanded and there is little evidence of agitation in the provinces. Abolitionism cannot have disappeared entirely, since it had been enthusiastically supported by so many, but holding meetings with a radical agenda soon fell outside of the law as the Pitt government enacted 'Gagging Acts' that extended the meaning of treason to include speaking and writing, even if no actions followed, and three local JPs were required to authorise all meetings of more than 50 people. The Newcastle Anti-Slavery Society seems to have disappeared after March 25, 1793.[17]

Revenge taken by the Black Army for the Cruelties practised on them by the French.

This disturbing graphic of the Haiti uprising goes some way towards explaining British fears of slave rebellion in the Caribbean.

3 The poet and the medical men

Talented and determined individuals, from different walks of life, had a great impact upon the growth of the movement for abolition.

Dozens of large meetings and thousands of petitioners can both reflect and shift public opinion. In the right circumstances they can influence or even change government policy. Forty years after the first movement was born, all of this actually happened. The other important ingredient for success is the impact of talented and determined individuals. Thomas Clarkson and William Wilberforce were the great national inspirations. The North East had its significant figures too. We have already introduced one, the indefatigable William Turner. The early movement had three more, James Stanfield, Thomas Trotter and Thomas Winterbottom.

James Field Stanfield was born in Dublin in 1749. In the early 1770s he went to sea in merchant ships and in 1774 he joined a slave ship sailing out

'Spanish Slave Brig, El Almirante', painted by Newcastle artist J.W. Carmichael (1799-1849). A brig is a two-masted vessel.

of Liverpool for Benin. He wrote a long poem, *Written on the West Coast of Africa 1776*.[18] He left the sea in 1777. There is no evidence that he voiced any hostility to the slave trade for another decade. He joined an acting troupe playing theatres along the North East coast from Scarborough to Sunderland, where he had settled. In 1788 he contacted Thomas Clarkson, who was compiling his great dossier on the slave trade, which he would soon present to a shocked and defensive parliament.[19]

Tyne and Wear Museums

James Field Stanfield, 1749-1824.

Stanfield wrote seven letters to Clarkson about the slave trade and their detail suggests that they were intended for publication. He showed how the circuit began in a dockside coffee house with discussion between merchants, agents and captains, who then moved out onto the streets to locate, flatter, traduce, inveigle or assault sailors into signing on for Africa-bound vessels. He asked why anyone should expect the truth from people who stood to gain at every stage in the gruesome business, but he also described the life of the common seamen, who were mercilessly flogged to the point of mutilation, and often death, in an orgy of sadistic cruelty. On arrival on the Guinea Coast they had to make exhausting preparations for the receipt of slaves who were then subjected to a routine of terror. Of his own vessel's crew of over 30 that left Liverpool, only five survived the first leg of the triangular voyage, and only two, the captain and Stanfield, made it back to Liverpool. The letters were published in a pamphlet, *Observations on a Guinea Voyage*, and reached a wide audience. Stanfield exploded the idea that the trade was a benign nursery for the Royal Navy and provided essential and telling propaganda for Clarkson and William Wilberforce, but the London Abolition Committee failed in their first attempts to effect change through Parliament in 1790.[20] In 1795 his long dramatic poem, *The Guinea Voyage*, was published in three volumes. It was a bad year for agitation and the full impact of the poem was probably delayed. Stanfield named his son after the leading abolitionist Thomas Clarkson, and he went on to become a celebrated painter, especially of marine scenes.

Thomas Trotter was born in the Scottish borders in 1760. He studied medicine and, in 1780, became a surgeon's mate on HMS *Berwick*, serving in the West Indies towards the end of the American War of Independence, where he must have witnessed the slave trade and slavery at first hand. In 1782 he was slightly wounded at sea, but was promoted to surgeon at the age of 21. The end of the war brought unemployment to many Royal Navy sailors, Trotter included, and in 1783, he sailed on what is now the most famous slave ship of all, the *Brooks* of Liverpool. (It was the subject of the illustration commissioned by Clarkson.) As ship's surgeon he was responsible for a cargo of slaves for 14 months. He vigorously challenged the owner on their conditions, but was ignored for reasons of cost. Nevertheless he played an important part in improving the health of all sea-

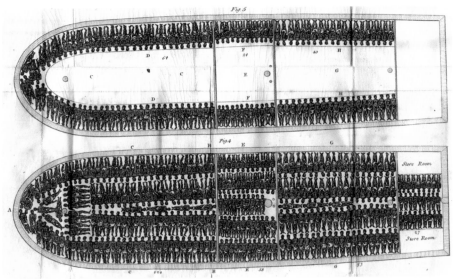

Newcastle Libraries (Clarkson's History of the Slave-Trade Vol II)

The illustration commissioned by Thomas Clarkson vividly shows the overcrowding of Africans on board the Brooks.

farers. In 1786 he published *Observations on the Scurvy* and was one of the major pioneers in the distribution of citrus juice throughout the Navy. He also researched the effects of drunkenness on the human body. He remained on call for the Navy, but became a prominent physician at Wooler in Northumberland, and then in Pilgrim Street, Newcastle. In 1789 he was among the Newcastle sponsors of the autobiography of a former slave, *The Interesting Narrative of the Life of Olaudah Equiano or Gustavus Vassa, the African*, which was published in London. In 1791 Dr Trotter was part of Turner's anti-slavery committee and also put his knowledge at Clarkson's disposal. In 1792 it was an invaluable part of the evidence that Clarkson presented to the Commons. Slave ships had a terrible reputation among sailors, and Clarkson revealed that on-board mortality was even greater among sailors than among slaves, thereby undermining the official view that slave ships were a tremendous training ground for the Navy.[21]

GUSTAVUS VASSA,

OR

Olaudah Equiano.

Escaped slave, Olaudah Equiano. He visited Newcastle in 1791.

Dr Thomas Winterbottom was born at South Shields in 1766. He studied medicine at Edinburgh and Glasgow and graduated in 1792. That August he arrived in Sierra Leone as the physician for a settlement of freed slaves established by abolitionists. He stayed four years and recorded his experiences. He was a pioneer of tropical medicine. One study laid out best medical practice for seamen and settlers, including a description of conditions on trading vessels. A second, published in 1803, described the physical state of Africans in Sierra Leone, including sleeping sickness.

Winterbottom used his first hand experience of Africans to contradict the stereotypes advanced by the apologists for slavery. He returned to North East England and practised as a physician in South Shields, where he campaigned for mine safety and a Mines Inspectorate and for better care of seamen and unmarried female servants. He founded the South Shields Marine School, which still survives, and actively supported all campaigns for the abolition of slavery. When he died in 1859 he was the oldest physician on the medical register.[22]

Dr Thomas Winterbottom.

Tyne and Wear Archives HO.ING/23/6

4 Abolition and the end of war

Britain was at war with France for 22 years from 1793, apart from a brief armistice in 1802. Severe repression of radical politics took place from the outbreak of war. Abolitionists were cowed and popular agitation came to an end. In 1807 deft handling in Parliament by Wilberforce, Grey and others pushed through legislation to end the slave trade in the British Empire. Attention shifted to the wider issues of slavery but despite a modest revival of mass activity at the end of the war, effective measures were deflected by a government fearful of rebellion at home and abroad and ready to act to stop it.

The leaders of the London Corresponding Society, including its Secretary, Thomas Hardy, Equiano's[23] friend, were indicted for treason, but were acquitted by a London jury to the dismay and anger of Attorney General, Sir John Scott.[24] London juries, socially broad in membership, were famed for their independence. In Scotland some fared worse. One man was hanged and others transported after being sentenced by the extremely vindictive Lord Justice Braxfield in Edinburgh.

Charles Grey,[25] MP for Northumberland, moved a motion for parliamentary reform in 1797. His prestige made him fire-proof in the Commons, but he wrote to his friend Sir John Swinburne, President of the Newcastle Literary and Philosophical Society, remarking that after the recent treason trials he could be the next to be indicted.

The Prime Minister, William Pitt, resigned when King George vetoed the Catholic Emancipation measure that had been promised in the 1801 Act of Union. There was a brief interlude in the war in 1802 – the Peace of Amiens – but it resumed in 1803 and the new Prime Minister, Henry Addington, mismanaged it. Napoleon was a military threat, but there was no longer a political threat to Britain, since his imperial designs were highly unattractive to the radicals who had survived Pitt's repressive policies. Pitt returned to office briefly in 1804 but died a year later in January 1806.

After several failed attempts during the 1790s, the leading abolitionist William Wilberforce aimed to outmanoeuvre the diehards of the West India parliamentary lobby and their friends. In 1806 the new government of Grenville and Fox included men with a strong commitment to abolition, though Wilberforce, Thomas Clarkson and James Stephen, the deft newcomer to abolitionist affairs, were at pains to move carefully. Stephen produced a formula that did not refer overtly to abolition but proposed to suppress the importation of slaves into new territories and thereby protect existing planters' interests. Enactment would mean stopping and searching enemy and neutral shipping, but for the patriots that was an attractive assertion of Britain's hegemony on the seas. The Fox-Grenville ministry was preoccupied with the implications of the continuing war, but fell apart in March as the abolition issue was being debated in Parliament, and Fox died in September.

The new government, led by the elderly and sick Duke of Portland, was fearful of unrest at home and embarked on a programme of barrack building in industrial areas. 12,000 soldiers were on the alert in the northern industrial towns. In 1807 the Newcastle guilds offered no encouragement to the local project, since the War Department coveted the Freemen's pasture, part of the Town Moor, but the Mayor and Common Council were sympathetic and the government got their barracks at Fenham. The army's presence may have acted as a deterrent to potential agitators.

Some of the strongest enemies of abolition in Parliament had gone, including several members of the West India lobby, and the 1801 Act of Union had produced a new block of Irish MPs. The abolition motion was presented in 1807 at a moment of national crisis. Napoleon was rampant on the Continent, the anti-French coalition had fractured, taxes and prices were rocketing and war weariness was endemic. The government needed an initiative to unite patriots, the peace faction, middle class reformers and those without a vote. Abolition of the slave trade was presented as a policy that gave Britain moral leadership in the world and damaged the economic prospects of its competitors. The motion swept

through both Houses of Parliament. The Newcastle papers published nothing about the machinations that led up to the Act, but quite long reports about the final debate in the Commons, where the motion was introduced by Charles Grey, now Lord Howick, and seconded by Ralph Milbanke, the MP for Durham, who had been a strong supporter of abolition since 1792.[26]

The 1807 Act outlawed the slave trade in the British Empire. In consequence British slave traders flew foreign flags and used routes below the Equator that were protected by the Spanish and Portuguese. The US Congress abandoned the trade in 1808, but American slavers operated secretly when possible, like their British counterparts. The London Abolition Committee became the African Institute enquiring into the state of Africa, but its members remained concerned over ongoing slave trade abuses. In 1810 the Institute suggested a law whereby slave owners would have to register their human property and their places of origin. The Institute envisaged an inspection by registration that would reveal anyone missing from the register and so indicate that they had been obtained illicitly.[27]

The war dragged on. The French Navy had suffered a conclusive defeat at sea at the Battle of Trafalgar in 1805, but Napoleon dominated the land war in Europe, registering great victories at Ulm in 1804, Austerlitz in 1806, Wagram in 1809 and the occupied Vienna in 1810. Despite imposing a blockade on Britain, Napoleon could not engineer an invasion, but strangling food supplies and causing bread shortages was a deeply serious business to a government anxious about unrest at home. In 1812 there were Luddite disturbances in the North and Midlands and a Liverpool merchant, whose business had been in trouble, assassinated the Prime Minister, Spencer Percival, in the House of Commons. However, Napoleon's armies were stretched as he attempted to keep and extend control in several theatres at the same time, and the breaking point came as his armies were depleted in the retreat from Moscow and then defeated in Northern Germany and Holland.

On December 22, 1813, 200 people sat down to a celebratory dinner at the Assembly Rooms in Westgate Street, Newcastle. 'The outside of the building was literally covered with variegated lamps, with the words "ORANGE BOVEN" in gilt letters.' ('Orange Boven' ['boven' = 'up'] was a

A

B I L L,

INTITULED,

An ACT for the Abolition of the Slave Trade.

Note.—*The Figures in the Margin denote the Number of the Presses in the Ingrossment.*

WHEREAS the *African* Slave Trade is contrary to the Principles of Justice, Humanity, and found Policy: *Preamble.*

And whereas the Two Houses of Parliament did, by their Resolutions of the tenth and twenty-fourth days of June one thousand eight hundred and six, severally resolve, That they, considering the *African* Slave Trade to be contrary to the Principles of Justice, Humanity, and found Policy, would, with all practicable Expedition, take effectual Measures for the Abolition of the said Trade, in such manner, and at such period as might be deemed adviseable :

And whereas it is expedient and adviseable that the same should be forthwith abolished and prohibited, and declared to be unlawful ;

Be it therefore Enacted by the KING's Most Excellent MAJESTY, by and with the Advice and Consent of the Lords Spiritual and Temporal, and Commons, in this present Parliament assembled, and by the Authority of the same, That from and after the first day of May one thousand eight hundred and seven, the *African* Slave Trade, and all and all manner of dealing and trading in the Purchase, Sale, Barter, or Transfer of Slaves, or of Persons intended to be sold, transferred, used, or dealt with as Slaves, practised or carried on, in, at, to, or from any part of the Coast or Countries of *Africa*, shall be, and the same is hereby utterly abolished, prohibited, and declared to be unlawful ; and also that all and all manner of dealing, either by way of Purchase, Sale, Barter, or Transfer, or by means of any other Contract or Agreement whatever, relating to any Slaves, or to any Persons intended to be used or dealt with as Slaves, for the purpose of such Slaves or Persons being removed or transported from any Island, Country, Territory, or Place whatever, in *Africa* or *The West Indies*, or in any other part of *America*, not being in the Dominion, Possession, or Occupation of His Majesty, to any other Island, Country, Territory, or Place whatever, is hereby in like manner utterly abolished, prohibited, and declared to be unlawful.

The African Slave Trade to be abolished after 1st of May 1807.

68.

And

reference to the restoration of the Dutch ruler). A similar event took place in Sunderland, but the celebrations were tempered on the 24th by an appalling disaster at Felling Colliery, when 22 men were killed outright and dozens were injured by an explosion in the shaft at shift change. This was less than a year after one of the worst pit disasters in the region's history, at the same colliery, when 91 men and boys died in an explosion.

Over New Year the Tyne was completely frozen at Newcastle.

> The temptation to indulge in skating was not to be resisted … [A Dutch
> seaman] put the strength of the ice to the test by passing over it with beef
> bones tied to the soles of his shoes and a long pole of wood in his hand, that
> in case the ice had broken he might have supported himself with the pole
> until assistance had been afforded him. Numbers soon ventured upon it.
> [Next day] 'the skaters were numerous and continued their diversion till the
> evening [and the river] continued to be covered with crowds of people … of
> all ages, ranks and sexes … several races took place for prizes … parties
> might be seen playing at foot-ball, quoits and in other directions, fruit and
> cake sellers, fiddlers, pipers, razor grinders, recruiting parties were to be met
> with … the whole scene resembled a country wake or fair or a race ground.

River navigation was impossible down to St Peter's Quay until early February 1814.

In April the allied armies moved on Paris, which fell on the 12th. In Durham town an effigy of Napoleon was mounted on an old horse and led through the streets to the market place and burned. Processions, parties and dinners were held in towns and villages across the region, no doubt expressing patriotic pride but also great relief at the ending of the generation-long war. In Newcastle on May 10 The Peace and Unity Hospital was opened. Reportedly, 40,000-50,000 people were in the streets and many had travelled miles to be there.

During the war economic downturns had borne really hard on poorer people's living standards. The availability and price of bread, the staple food, was a serious matter. Such a downturn had begun in 1812 and in May 1814, before the harvest, and in only three days 11,500 Newcastle people signed petitions to Parliament demanding that the government keep the corn laws in place.

Across the country the Anti-Slavery Committees rapidly revived and 841 petitions, carrying 755,000 signatures – more than in 1791-2 – were submitted to Parliament in one month. On June 17 the Newcastle abolitionists agreed to send requests to sign petitions across the region. On the 24th a resolution was sent to Hexham's Chief Magistrate and to other towns. On the 29th a large meeting, presided over by the Newcastle Mayor, Thomas Smith, adopted several resolutions including the London Meeting resolution calling for repression of French slave trading. A large Anti-Slavery Committee was established to prepare petitions. Several veterans of 1791 were present, including the Unitarians William Turner and William Batson, and the Quakers Robert Ormston, Hadwen Bragg, Anthony Clapham, Jonathan Priestman, George Richardson. The Baptist John Fenwick, plus the Reverends Davison, Pringle and Pengelly, whose denominations are not known, also attended. Joseph Clark was also involved. (He had become a thorn in the Common Council's flesh by alleging their corruption.) There were also the merchants Nicholas

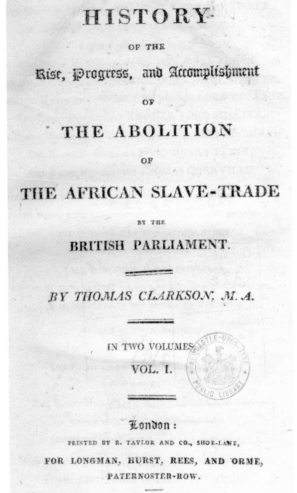

Newcastle Libraries (Clarkson's History of the Slave-Trade Vol II)

HISTORY

OF THE

Rise, Progress, and Accomplishment

OF

THE ABOLITION

OF

THE AFRICAN SLAVE-TRADE

BY THE

BRITISH PARLIAMENT.

BY THOMAS CLARKSON, M.A.

IN TWO VOLUMES.

VOL. I.

London:

PRINTED BY R. TAYLOR AND CO., SHOE-LANE,

FOR LONGMAN, HURST, REES, AND ORME,

PATERNOSTER-ROW.

1808.

In 1808 Clarkson dedicated his history to Lord Grenville, Earl Grey, and a further seven cabinet ministers of the 'wise and virtuous administration' who had steered the Act through Parliament.

Newcastle during the Napoleonic Wars, around 1807.

Naters, Robert Doubleday and Robert Rankin. The latter was the proprietor of a sugar house, the grandfather of Harriet Martineau, and, like Doubleday, a Unitarian. A former Newcastle Mayor, Archibald Reed, was present, as was James Angas, the coach builder. It was a formidable section of Newcastle's middle class and several of them were active in the Literary and Philosophical Society. They had weathered the difficult war years and were once more ready and able to speak out publicly.[28] The 1791 veterans believed their work directly impacted on policy more than it had done in the earlier campaign.

After the Peace of Paris in 1814 the British government's position changed. At the Congress of Vienna in 1815 it was determined that French colonies would not be permitted to import slaves. Since the US government had outlawed the trade, it was brought to an end north of the Equator, though freebooters tried to continue working on the route to Brazil. Caribbean and North American planters were against the trade, if not on moral grounds, then to suppress competition from the Spanish and Portuguese planter economy. The final act was played out by the British Navy on the West African Coast and in Caribbean waters. Capture of slave ships under any colours had dire consequences for British and American captains and owners, including imprisonment and transportation, and the slaves were normally returned to Africa.[29]

Post-war demobilisation brought widespread unemployment and a level of desperation to North East working-class communities. The labour market was flooded with former Navy men and employers took the opportunity to drive down pay and conditions. In the early autumn of 1815, merchant seamen closed the major rivers and halted the coal trade. This very bitter dispute caused dangerous divisions in the local communities. Troops were moved up from Yorkshire and a naval squadron was stationed at the mouth of the Tyne. When the dispute ended after six weeks, numerous arrests were made, but the long gap between arrest and trial probably tempered the severity of the sentences. Elsewhere in Britain dissent was often met with much greater savagery from a ruling elite determined to hold the line from a rising tide of popular protest, but skilled seamen's labour power was a vital commodity in the North East and keeping them relatively content was economically essential.

There was still a vigorous market in slaves between Caribbean islands, even though this was forbidden under the 1807 British Act, and there was still buying and selling on the islands and in the United States and South America. The abolitionist campaign in Britain shifted from the slave trade to the institution of slavery itself, though this exposed differences in the movement (mostly concerned with the method and pace of 'manumission' – the voluntary freeing of slaves – and registration) it was both attainable and less controversial. In 1817 manumission was enacted by Orders in Council, but responsibility was entrusted to colonial administrations. The British abolitionist movement lost focus and declined, partly because of differences within the leadership over the next steps to be taken, but mainly because of the general fate

Sourced at Library of Congress

Slaves for sale at Ashley Ferry, outside Charleston, South Carolina, c.1780s.

of radical opinion in the years following the end of the war.

August 1819 saw the Peterloo Massacre in Manchester, when local Yeomanry savagely attacked a peaceful mass demonstration for suffrage reform. The events leading up to it, including agitation, arrests, changes in the law and punitive sentences, and the consequences of the massacre meant that only the most courageous – or foolhardy – radicals were prepared to speak out. Even Lord Lambton (known as Radical Jack), scion of one of Durham's leading families, was threatened with arrest. Many abolitionists, like Wilberforce, did not wish to be associated in any way with radical agitation. Meanwhile, the profits of slavery continued to be enjoyed by traders and plantation owners.

Tyne and Wear Museums

AFRICAN SLAVE TRADE.

WE, the undersigned, request a Meeting of the Inhabitants of the Town and neighbourhood of Sunderland, at the EXCHANGE, on Saturday, July the 2d, at 11 o'Clock in the Forenoon, to take into consideration the propriety of petitioning the Legislature, in consequence of the avowed intention, on the part of France, to renew the AFRICAN SLAVE TRADE ; and also to consider of such other measures as may be expedient, to support the present exertions of MR. WILBERFORCE, in effecting its entire Abolition.

J. Hampson, M. A.	R. Milbanke
John Croudace	John Davison
Rob. Davidson	Bernard Ogden
W. Walton	G. W. Meadley
Thomas Robson	A. Fenwick
R. Fenwick	Thomas Young
I. Ayton	H. Fearon, M. D.
Ralph Carr	J. Armstrong, M.D.
Mich. Longridge	John Lotherington
	John White

June 29th. 1814,

The inhabitants of Sunderland met to protest against Louis XVIII's reinstatement of the slave trade in France in 1815. Pressure from Britain forced him to back down later.

5 Mitigating and gradually abolishing ...

After decades of passivity the popular abolitionist movement sprang to life in the 1820s as part of a general revival of radical politics. In the first instance it was largely cautious in practice and moderate in objective though a minority began to press for total abolition.

In the spring of 1820 'mad' King George died after 60 years on the throne. His death began to break the reactionary log jam of the previous quarter of a century. The new King, George IV, was noted for his lascivious life style and wanted Parliament to sanction his separation from Queen Caroline on the grounds of her alleged adultery. 'The Queen Caroline Affair' became the subject of vicious infighting among the ruling elite, caused satirical delight in the underground press, and prompted pro-Queen mass demonstrations across the country.[30] Whig politicians used the issue to attack the Tory government without risking being called unpatriotic. The Queen's advisor, Henry Brougham, had been an abolitionist since 1804, and even the Tory, William Wilberforce, was engaged with the issue. Radicals of all stripes, including the firmest republicans, defended the Queen with gusto. It was their first opportunity for a generation to get onto the streets without facing army sabres. The government was forced to back away from a Commons Bill supporting the King, and when it fell there were national celebrations.

Newcastle and Gateshead streets 'were brilliantly illuminated as a testimony of joy on the abandonment of the Bill against her majesty Queen Caroline' and 'devices and transparencies were exhibited in various parts of the town' with mottos such as 'Long live Queen Caroline', 'Innocence triumphant' and 'Earl Grey for ever'.[31] A recent law restricting the right of assembly and aimed at strangling political dissent was simply ignored. The old political issues, and some newer ones, were on the agenda, including the Test Acts, Catholic Emancipation, parliamentary reform, the Combination Acts and the abolition of slavery. The slavery question was rather less dangerous than the others, since many of its supporters were members of the elite and so to some extent politically protected.

It had been a decade since their last successful public campaign and news from the colonies had piled up in the press. Planters were ignoring or trying to subvert slave registration. The treatment of slaves may even have deteriorated since 1807. Unable to purchase new slaves legally, planters worked the slaves they had harder. Missionary endeavours had increased, but local authorities stopped them preaching to slaves, and the missionaries' accounts of this were devoured by a wide and concerned public in Britain.

Cane cutters in the Caribbean.

It was a year or two before the resignations or deaths of leading members of the reactionary political elite – notably Sidmouth, Liverpool and Castlereagh, who were closely associated with the war-time and post war repression – helped to break the ice. Economic recovery also played a part.

Among the veteran abolitionists, William Wilberforce and James Stephen remained important. A revitalised 64-year-old Thomas Clarkson undertook another physically onerous tour of Britain and covered 3,000 miles in six months, but leadership was passing to a younger generation. Wilberforce had asked Henry Brougham and Thomas Fowell Buxton[32] to take up the campaign in Parliament. Attention shifted from the slave trade to the state of slavery, and the intention was to press Parliament into legislating for improvements in conditions. Zachary Macaulay, using his experience as a plantation overseer, had assiduously pursued information from the colonies.

In January 1823 the National Society for Mitigating and Gradually Abolishing the State of Slavery throughout the British Dominions was founded. Its ponderous name indicated the caution and ambiguity of a movement that had been on hold for a decade. The word 'gradually' incensed many abolitionists, but others felt that proceeding 'gradually' might have a better chance of getting legislation through Parliament, and once that was achieved they could press for more. Some abolitionists actually feared immediate abolition, because they believed that slaves were infantile, unready and insufficiently infused with Christian virtues, so a good dose of

Anti-Slavery International

William Wilberforce.

missionary attention was required first. Some were terrified by the potential violence of a people who had lived such submissive existences without the benefits of Christian education.[33]

Nevertheless, the founding of the Society elicited an enormous response. In the first year of its existence, 220 local societies were founded or reconstituted and 825 petitions were sent to Parliament. (In 1824 there were to be 674.) Anti-slavery had become firmly lodged in the country's political culture and North East England was no exception. The Reverend James Collinson of Gateshead Parish Church had been in the forefront of the 1814 agitation and had organised a committee of 12 to promote a petition against the resumption of the French slave trade. Early in May 1823 he was back on the war path, hosting a meeting for a Gateshead Petition for the Abolition of Slavery through the British Dominions. Petitions were also sent from Alnwick, Blyth, Hexham, Newcastle, Tynemouth, Jarrow, South Shields, Sunderland, Chester-le-Street, Durham, Darlington, Barnard Castle,

Stockton and tiny, remote, Staindrop. There was no hint of 'gradually' there.

The King's speech to Parliament in 1824 had advocated moderate improvements to the conditions of slaves. Thomas Buxton put a motion to Parliament calling for gradual abolition. In order to sidetrack this initiative, on May 13 the government issued Orders in Council requiring colonial assemblies to enact ameliorative measures, including stopping enslaved women being lashed, but voices in the colonies were resistant.

The Newcastle meeting on May 14 constituted itself as The Newcastle Society for Mitigating and Gradually Abolishing the State of Slavery throughout the British Dominions. James Losh was the major spokesman, and he appears to have formulated the resolutions that echo the moderation of the London Committee. William Turner provided a link with 1791 in seconding them.[34]

The Reverend John Smith of the London Missionary Society had gone to Demerara, British Guiana, in 1817. Against the wishes and pressure of the planters he preached to slaves and drew them into congregations outside their workplaces. They acquired self respect and the opportunity to communicate with other slaves across the colony. Smith strongly advised against rebellion, but the rapid spread of evangelical Christianity bore fruit, if not quite as he had intended.

In August 1823, slaves in Demerara learned that Parliament's modest proposed measures were being withheld. 12,000 of them refused to work and marched to Georgetown, the capital, to protest, with

Newcastle Literary and Philosophical Society

James Losh.

Northumberland Collections Service (SANT-BEQ-26-01-01-027)

Gateshead Petition

FOR THE

Abolition of Slavery.

AT A MEETING of the Inhabitants of the Parish of Gateshead, in the County of Durham, and its Vicinity, held at the Anchorage, on the 2nd Day of May, 1823, for the Purpose of taking into Consideration, the Propriety of Petitioning Parliament to take such Measures as may be most condusive to the Mitigation and ultimate Abolition of Slavery throughout the British Dominions.

The Rev. JOHN COLLINSON, Rector, in the Chair.

The following Petition was unanimously approved of and adopted:

To the Honorable the COMMONS of the united Kingdom of Great Britain and Ireland, in Parliament assembled.

The Petition of the undersigned Inhabitants of the Parish of Gateshead, in the County of Durham, and its Vicinity,

humbly sheweth,

That your Petitioners, feeling as Christians, most deeply and sincerely deplore the debased, degraded and miserable condition of the numerous Human Beings who are held in a State of Slavery, by Subjects of His Majesty in Colonies belonging to the British Empire, a State in direct Opposition to the Principles of Christianity, and highly aggravated by the Cruelties, Deprivations and other manifold but, unhappily, too well known Evils, revolting to Humanity, to which those unfortunate Creatures are, their Treatment, subjected.

That your Petitioners, in common with a great Proportion of His Majesty's Subjects, are impressed with an ardent desire that the Sufferings of those unhappy Slaves may be alleviated, and their Condition so far ameliorated, as that they may be encouraged in their Efforts to obtain their Freedom, and that when obtained, they may afterwards securely enjoy the Benefits resulting from it.

That encouraged by the Sympathy which has at all Times been evinced by His Majesty's Government, in behalf of Sufferers of every Description, and not less so, by its laudable Example and benevolent Efforts, for the total and universal Abolition of the Slave Trade; your Petitioners humbly presume, in conjunction with His Majesty's other Subjects, whose Motives and Object are the same, most earnestly to implore your honourable House, to adopt such Measures, as to its Wisdom shall seem most Proper, effectually to remedy the Evils of that Slavery, under which so many Human Beings are at present suffering; and thereby enable the unfortunate and unhappy Creatures, forming the Slave Population, in His Majesty's Colonies, to enjoy the Rights and Privileges common to Mankind, from a Participation of which, they are inhumanly, and as your Petitioners humbly conceive, and thus venture to state, unjustly excluded.

And your Petitioners will ever Pray, &c.

And the Inhabitants of Gateshead and its Vicinity, are respectively informed that the Petition will lie for Signatures at the Goat Inn, and at the Shops of Mr Greene, and Mr Colman, until Monday next at 12 o'Clock.

By Order of the Committee,

THOMAS SWINBURNE, Secretary.

GATESHEAD, 2nd MAY, 1823.

Akenheads, Printers, Newcastle.

captive whites in tow. The demonstrators were unarmed, and did very little violence to white people, yet troops gunned down hundreds of them and hunted others. Thirty were tried, executed and their heads stuck on pikes. Many of the leading slaves were the most committed black Christians. Smith was charged with treason, convicted and condemned to death. He sent a plea for pardon to London, but died from pneumonia in prison before it arrived.[35]

In October chapels in Barbados were attacked. On January 30, 1824, a Newcastle newspaper reported:

> The people of Barbados have issued a declaration against that of the Governor respecting them pulling down the chapel of Mr Shrewsbury, the Methodist preacher, in which they declare that the outrage was committed by persons of the greatest respectability and that their object was to eradicate Methodism ... [concluding] With a fixed determination therefore to put an end to Methodism in this island; all Methodist preachers are warned not to approach these shores; as if they do, it will be at their own peril.

Slave rebellions in Jamaica and St Kitts were thwarted and alleged leaders punished, yet the real rebels were the planters who were determined to ignore Parliament's moderate measures.

On February 7 the same Newcastle newspaper reported from Kingston, Jamaica.

> The assembly have passed a resolution annulling the registration bill. It is of course anticipated that the Governor will not sanction this bill and that it will remain a dead letter. In the meantime comes the question of the expenses of the Registration which every three years costs around £3000. Depend upon it this supply will be refused by the assembly in which case there will be open warfare between the Governor and the assembly.

On March 27 the Newcastle newspaper quoted an anonymous source in Jamaica:

> I hope all will pass over without disturbance to the place or the island; but it is the decided opinion of everyone here that if the government at home agitate the question of emancipation of the slaves we shall have a revolution in the island as it is. You can purchase property at almost any rate.

*A detail from a map of the Caribbean in Hewson Clarke's 'History of the War',
1816. (Newcastle Libraries)*

There was a large reading public in and around Newcastle. The *Tyne
Mercury* was radical in its ownership and politics. Presumably William
Mitchell, the owner-editor, believed his readers wanted such news, though
perhaps he was trying to educate them about the slave system, and to arm
them, so they would take up the case for abolition. His middle-class readers
may have been cautious, and even fearful, about the consequences of black
rebellion, but would also condemn the behaviour of colonial whites as
related to them both by the press and by the pastors whose missions they
supported financially. The Newcastle Society appears to have remained
moderate. Late in March a Newcastle paper reported that Losh had called
for an amelioration of the working conditions of the slaves but emphasised
that, in his view, 'the Moral Character of the Negro Slave' was 'not Now in
a Condition to receive the Blessing of Liberty'. The Newcastle Society may
have met in 1824 and 1825, but it was not reported in the local press.

During the General Election campaign of 1826, a candidate, Mr Powlett
was reported as saying that he had 'uniformly supported' motions against
slavery and on a future occasion, 'if he found the government was insincere,

then he would take up the cause which was that of Parliament and the people of England, and say that those resolutions must be carried into effect.'

Thomas Wentworth Beaumont[36] declared that he was standing on 'Anti-ministerial political principles …' and his central policy was 'total extinction of slavery.' He was no less forthright at Alnwick hustings:

> I am anxious for the speedy and entire abolition of slavery. I am not satisfied with the conduct of the Administration on that topic. They talk about the necessity of paying attention to vested interests but they overlook the vested interests which each man has in happiness and liberty. The vested interest of the slave in his own freedom is much higher than the vested interest in the worth of that slave. I will not be satisfied till they raise the Negro from that state of beasts of burden, and place them in a situation of men and free men. This is my opinion respecting that question, and I shall leave it there, having pledged myself to support the entire and speedy abolition of slavery.

A 'Newcastle Whig' saw the election as an opportunity to repay Earl Grey for his contribution to the abolition campaign by voting for his son, Lord Howick, 'The determined Enemy of Slavery'.

At Alnwick hustings, the Hon H.T. Liddell, the Tory, said:

> I have been asked if I was friendly to slavery. I am astonished that such a question can be put to an Englishman. For my part, I earnestly hope to witness the day, when this disgraceful traffic will be for ever abolished and extinguished, and that wherever the sun sets on our most distant colonies, the inhabitants will be happy free men. But gentlemen, there is considerable danger in any precipitate change, and on this particular subject the utmost calmness is required, and must necessarily be maintained by all who value the security of our colonies, the rights of property, and the welfare of the slaves themselves.

Liddell was elected, but in his maiden speech to the Commons he said nothing about slavery.[37]

Silence on the abolition question was not an option. Even those who were unwilling to support abolitionist bills felt bound to condemn the slavery system in principle. Yet the meandering confrontation between the Colonial Office and the planters dominated colonial assemblies and dampened the campaign in Britain. It failed to find a focus. Meanwhile radicals were distracted by the battles to end to the Test Acts and bring about Catholic Emancipation. Progress had always been difficult under Tory governments because they were usually sympathetic to the planter interest in the West Indies and to absentee plantation owners in Britain.

Continuity of personnel between each stage of the long campaign was very important but each stage brought new people into the movement. In the 1820s Christopher Wawn, a Newcastle surgeon, took up the cause. His special contribution to the anti-slavery issue lay in his dispute with Lord Stowell (William Scott), another Newcastle man and, like his brother Lord Eldon, a senior judge. In 1827 Wawn wrote a pamphlet challenging Stowell's judgment that a slave called Grace would be free whilst in England but return to slave status when she went back to Antigua. The planters had taken the Stowell judgement as an affirmation of their property rights in human beings. Wawn took the view that holding people in bondage only stored up problems which would ultimately rebound against the country. He suggested that slaves in British colonies might look up to the example of Haiti; a radical observation indeed.[38]

The engraved image of a slave, right, by Thomas Bewick, was frequently reproduced as a 'logo' by abolitionists along with the motto 'Am I Not a Man and a Brother'. The image was used on many anti-slavery tracts including the 1791 Newcastle edition of Thomas Clarkson's Abstract (page 27). There is a dispute as to whether the image was first designed by potter Josiah Wedgewood for a medallion produced in 1787, or by Bewick. Both were involved in the abolition movement. Coins and medals bearing the image were widely distributed. Above, left, is a copper halfpenny.

6 Every slave ... shall be free

For the first time since the 1790s a mass movement began to emerge in London and the provinces in 1830. Within this movement a growing minority called for a complete end to slavery. It took place against a gathering crisis in British society.

On May 15, 1830, the London Anti-Slavery Committee held its annual meeting at the Freemason's Hall. George Stephen, a younger son of the veteran abolitionist James Stephen, had been trying without success to encourage friends of abolition to attend the Committee for years, but now:

> This enormous Hall was crammed to suffocation, hundreds were turned away at the doors, and yet 2000 people were said to be present. Wilberforce was in the chair; nobility and gentlemen, of pre-eminent distinction supported him on every side, and Brougham, Buxton, Denman, Lushington and O'Connell[39] were among the speakers. It was a goodly, a magnificent spectacle! Well do I remember saying to those around me what I sincerely felt – 'today the slave is free!' and all appeared to share the same feeling.

Yet they were divided over the extent and speed of emancipation and 'the very demon of procrastination seemed to have possessed the leaders. A string of resolutions was proposed by Buxton; admirably worded; admirably indignant, but – admirably prudent!' An angry young delegate moved an amendment:

> in a few pithy words, deprecating indecision and delay [and insisting] 'that from and after the first of January, 1831, every slave on, or within the King's dominions shall be free.' It was a spark to the mine! Shouts, the tumult of applause was such as I never heard before, and never shall hear again. Cheers innumerable thundered from every bench, hats and handkerchiefs were waved in every hand.[40]

George IV died in June and his death precipitated a general election, which was to take place in September. In July the Bourbon monarchy fell in France.

On August 11 there was a meeting in the Brunswick Chapel, Newcastle,

AT

A SPECIAL GENERAL MEETING

Of the Newcastle Upon Tyne

ANTI-SLAVERY SOCIETY

Held in Brunswick Place Chapel, on Wednesday, the 11th of August, 1830, for the Purpose of considering the present State of the NEGRO POPULATION in the West Indies, and the propriety of Petitioning Parliament on the Subject.

Thomas Wentworth Beaumont, Esq., M. P.

VICE PRESIDENT, IN THE CHAIR.

On a Motion by Henry Brougham, Esq., M. P. seconded by Dr. Headlam, It was unanimously resolved,—

That this Meeting deeply regrets that the Resolutions respecting the Amelioration of the Slave Population, and the gradual Extinction of Slavery in the British Colonies, unanimously passed by the House of Commons, on the 15th May, 1923, and Afterwards adopted by the House of Lords, should have remained nearly a dead Letter, and that no effectual Measures should yet have been taken to deliver our beloved Country from the foul Crime of holding 800,000 of our unoffending Fellow-Subjects in the Fetters of one of the most degraded and detestable States of Bondage, to which any portion of the Human Species has ever been Subject.

On a Motion by John Hodgson, Esq. M. P. seconded by John Grey, Esq., It was unanimously resolved,—

That this Meeting is of opinion, that it is in vain to look to the Colonial Legislatures, or to any Orders of Council, however well intentioned, for a Mitigation of the Evils, and the gradual Extinction of Slavery in the British Dominions. and that the only hope which the Friends of the Negro Race can cherish is in the Wisdom and Justice of the Imperial Parliament, to extend the Blessings of Civil and Religious Liberty to every Section of the Empire.

On a Motion by Mr John Fenwick, seconded by the Rev. Christopher Bird, It was unanimously resolved,—

First,—That this Meeting is of opinion, that if it should be deemed inexpedient at once to manumit the Slave Population, yet means should immediately be taken, to annex the Slaves to the Plantations where they are at present located—to prevent the compulsory Separation of Families—to secure to the Slaves the Rights of Person and of Property—and the effectual Administration of Justice—to entitle them to the Rest of the Christian Sabbath—to give them one Working Day in the Week for their own Benefit—to promote Marriage among them—to facilitate Manumissions—and to allow the entire Slave Population the full Benefit of Christian Instruction, and especially that all Negro Children, to be born after an early Day, shall be declared free, and the care of their Nurture and Education be undertaken by the State.

Second,—That Petitions founded on the forgoing Resolutions, be prepared in Order to their being presented to both Houses of Parliament—That the Petition to the Lords be presented by Earl Grey, and that to the Commons, by the Members for Newcastle upon Tyne.

Third,—That Copies of these Resolutions be transmitted to the Dukes Northumberland and Portland—to the Marquesses of Londonderry and Cleveland—to the Earls of Carlisle, Tankerville, Grey and Eldon—to Lords Redesdale, Ravensworth, Stowell, and Durham—to the Lord Bishop of Durham—and to the Members for Newcastle, Northumberland, and Durham,—with a Request that they will Support, in Parliament, the Prayer of the Petition to be presented.

Fourth,—That the word "gradual" be omitted in the Title of the Society.

Fifth,—That it is expedient to promote Ladies' Anti-Slavery Societies ; and that it be an Instruction to the Committee to adopt such Measures as may be likely to accomplish their Institution in this part of the Country.

Sixth,—That the cordial thanks of this Meeting be given to Mr. Brougham for his exertions in the Cause of Civil and Religious Liberty all over the World, and especially for his presence on this occasion.

Seventh,—That the cordial thanks of this Meeting be given to the Trustees of Brunswick-Place Chapel for the kind and friendly manner in which they granted the use of the Chapel for the Meeting.

Mr. Beaumont having left the Chair:

On a Motion by John Hodgson, Esq. M. P. seconded by the Rev. W. H. Stowell, It was unanimously resolved,—

That the cordial thanks of this Meeting be given to Mr Beaumont, for his Readiness in accepting, and his able conduct in the Chair.

MATTHEW FORSTER, ⎰
JOHN FENWICK, ⎱ SECRETARIES.

⁎⁎ **PETITIONS to both Houses of Parliament in accordance with the foregoing Resolutions, are now lying for Signature at Mr. Charnley's, in the Bigg Market, Mr. Geo. Richardson's, in Union Street, at Messrs Finlay and Charlton's, in Pilgrim Street, and at Mr Joseph Clark's, Newgate Street.**

J. Clark, Printer, 11, Newgate Street, Newcastle.

the new citadel of Wesleyan Methodism. The principal speaker, Henry Brougham, MP, had been a leading parliamentarian and advocate of anti-slavery measures for 30 years, and he was also a friend of James Losh. The first motion, moved by Brougham and seconded by Dr Thomas Headlam, the town's medical officer, proposed that 'this meeting deeply regrets that the resolutions respecting the amelioration of the slave population and the gradual extinction of slavery in the British colonies unanimously passed by the House of Commons' had ' remained a dead letter' and 'no effectual measures have yet been taken to deliver ... 800,000 of our fellow subjects in the fetters of the most degradable and detestable states of bondage.' The second motion was moved by John Hodgson, MP for County Durham, and seconded by John Grey of Dilston. It proposed that 'this meeting is of the opinion that it is in vain to look for the colonial legislators or any Orders of Council however well intended, for a mitigation of the evils and the gradual extinction of slavery in the British dominions.'

The third motion was moved by John Fenwick, a strongly committed abolitionist, and the Reverend Christopher Bird from Durham Cathedral. It argued for immediately annexing slaves to their plantations, preventing families being broken up by sales, securing the slaves' rights of person and property, allowing them to rest on the Christian Sabbath, allowing one day a week to work for their own benefit, promoting marriage, allowing the benefit of Christian instruction, making manumission easier, setting free immediately all black children born after a certain date and making the state responsible for their nurture and education. The word 'Gradually' should be removed from the Newcastle Society's title, there should be local Ladies' Antislavery Societies and petitions to both houses of Parliament, including all these points, should be placed at several town booksellers for signature.[41] The prominence of the speakers, the attendance and the comprehensive nature of the business strongly suggest that this was not simply a Newcastle meeting, but a regional one, designed to spread the agitation.

From summer to autumn there was revolt in the countryside, especially in the South East. Ricks were burned, fences broken and threshing machines smashed. Special commissions handed out severe punishments. Then there was an outbreak of cholera beginning in Sunderland, which was particularly hard hit.

In September the Tories were re-elected. In the King's speech debate, the new Prime Minister, the crusty Duke of Wellington, insisted that not an inch would be given by way of parliamentary reform. He delighted his extremist supporters. Yet many Tory MPs could not forgive him for conceding Catholic Emancipation the year before, and he could not rely on them for support, so his government was very unstable. Some parliamentary supporters of the West Indian interest believed that they had most to lose from the abolition of slavery. They were also among those who had to most to lose from the Whigs' reform proposals, including the axing of over 150 rotten borough seats and the allocation of a similar number to new towns and bigger county electorates. Abolition and parliamentary reform were also connected through a distinct, though not precisely defined, feeling that the moment for 'reform' in general had arrived. The Whig Earl Grey, a man in his late sixties but the most confident of aristocrats and a parliamentary reformer and abolitionist since the 1780s, worked to preserve the dominance of the aristocratic elite by sharing power with new money when necessary and also by trying to create a loyal middle class.[42]

During September and October anti-slavery meetings were held in Bishop Auckland, Darlington, Durham, Sunderland, South Shields, North Shields, Hexham, Alnwick and Berwick. Late in October, Morpeth abolitionists announced that:

Morpeth market place in the early 19th century.

Newcastle Libraries (local colour prints)

A Meeting will be held in the Independent Chapel on Monday the 1st day of November next, at 6 o'clock in the evening, to adopt such measures as may appear most expedient to procure the abolition of Slavery in our colonies.

Dr Headlam of Newcastle was there and the meeting agreed that:

a state of personal slavery appears to this meeting to be repugnant to reason, to the spirit of the Christian religion, and to the genius of the British Constitution and opposed to every principle of natural law, in as much as no human legislature has any lawful power to abridge the natural rights of life or liberty, unless the owner shall himself commit or be charged with the commission of some act that amounts to a forfeiture thereof.

William Woodman, secretary of the Morpeth Anti-Slavery Society, photographed in old age.

Those present also insisted that 'all children born after a day to be named by parliament should be at once declared free. And that at the earliest period consistent with the general welfare and safety of the community, slavery should cease in any form to exist within the limits of the British dominions.' They proposed that 'a society be immediately formed in this town to promote the abolition of slavery in our colonies' and that 'the Right Hon[ora]ble Earl Grey be requested to become patron of the society. The Hon the Viscount Morpeth president, The Hon the Viscount Howick, the members for the county, the members for the borough and W.E.H. Ord Esq. MP, vice presidents and that the thanks of this meeting be at the same time given to these individuals for the exertions they have hitherto made in the cause of humanity.' Finally it was agreed that 'petitions founded upon these resolutions be addressed to both houses of parliament. And that Lord Grey be requested to present that to the house of Lords. And that the members for the borough be requested to present and support that to the House of Commons.' Copies of these resolutions were to be 'immediately transmitted' to local dignitaries.

William Woodman, a solicitor and Town Clerk, and Secretary of the Morpeth Anti-Slavery Society, sent the resolutions to Earl Grey, who replied a fortnight later.

> It can hardly be necessary for me to say that I certainly concur in all the feelings expressed by the respectable members, who composed that meeting, with respect to Negro slaves ... I feel at the same time the necessity of great caution in the measures which may be required for the accomplishment of that object ... and I am not quite prepared to say that I could at once agree to so early & divisive a measure as that which appears to have been approved by the meeting ... On this account, & having for some time withdrawn myself from all association of the same nature with that which it is now proposed to form, I feel myself under the necessity of declining the high & honourable station in it, which has been offered to me.

Grey's son, Lord Howick was also cautious:

> I regret that it is not in my power to become one of their vice presidents. I am as adverse as any one to the system of slavery, & shall always be ready to support in my place in parliament any well considered scheme for putting an end to it, but as I doubt whether the societies which are now forming are calculated to promote the temperate discussion of the question, I have resolved not to belong to any of them.

He evidently had the Reform Bill riots very much in mind.[43]

Other replies were more positive. William Ord, MP, a 'left wing' Whig, the Earl of Tankerville, the Earl of Carlisle and Viscount Morpeth, his son, all of whose families had had strong plantation interests, accepted the honorary positions and agreed to carry the petition to Parliament. It bore 200 names, a considerable number from such a small borough as Morpeth.[44]

By November, Wellington could not hold his MPs in line and had to resign. Earl Grey was Prime Minister by late December, and Brougham was Chancellor of the Exchequer. Both were abolitionists. During 1831 the

North East pitmen were on strike, and threatening property. They won, but when they struck again in 1832 they were defeated.

By spring 1831 Buxton had delivered over 500 abolitionist petitions to the Commons, but Grey and his ministers seemed not to be interested. Grey's government focussed on reform of the Poor Law, factory legislation and the National Debt, and on the biggest reform of all – on which all the others, including the abolition of slavery, appeared to depend – reforming Parliament by abolishing rotten boroughs, widening the franchise and rectifying demographic, geographical and social imbalances. On March 1 Grey's government put a Reform Bill to Parliament. It had been a very closely guarded secret and the Commons was shocked. Among the 168 seats to be abolished were those of the bulk of the West Indian interest, yet the Tory managers let the first reading go unchallenged.

In April Viscount Howick reported that ministers could offer no new proposals on the slavery question. (His father, Grey, thought him over zealous about the cause.) George Stephen felt that anti-slavery sentiment was 'in suspended animation', but a noisy annual meeting of the Anti-Slavery Committee at Exeter Hall, London, on the 23rd, issued a unanimous call for 'immediate abolition of colonial slavery.'[45] Furious with slow progress some abolitionists formed a breakaway 'ginger' group, 'The Agency Committee'.[46] Evidence of North Easterners' involvement has not come to light but its central policy of an end to gradualism was influential in the region.

In spring and summer MPs were almost entirely occupied with the Reform Bill. It was carried by a sizeable majority and went to the Lords in September. On November 8 it was defeated there by 41 votes. This provoked peaceful mass meetings in towns and villages across the country, but large-scale riots in Bristol, Nottingham and London. The crisis dragged on over the winter recess and the anti-slavery question became a sideshow.

Northumberland Collections Service (SANT-BEQ-04-14-041b)

Henry Grey, Viscount Howick.

7 An insurrection among the slaves

In 1831 full scale rebellion broke out in Jamaica. At home abolitionists were confused and divided until news reached them of planter reprisals. Meanwhile the British crisis deepened and abolition became tangled in the great debate over parliamentary reform. The Reform Bill slowly made its way through parliament and the anti-slavery agitators believed that the Grey government was stalling on its promises to deal with the slavery. Vast petitions were organised and the government came forward with an abolition bill. The enormous celebrations were dampened somewhat by a growing awareness of the details of the legislation.

Trouble had been brewing for some time in Jamaica. There had been a steady fall in slave numbers since 1807, but sugar prices and profits had fallen, so slaves were worked harder and harder, despite the British Parliament's recommendation of 1824 that planters should treat slaves more humanely. Political consciousness among the slaves had grown. They knew about the debates in Britain. Small shifts towards better treatment, and proposals to free the slaves, were often interpreted as a British initiative. That view was encouraged by the teachings of Baptist and Methodist missionaries. In December 1831 the word spread through plantations around Montego Bay in the north of the island that slaves would not return to work after Christmas. Just before Christmas a major slave rebellion broke out. Work stopped and some masters' property and persons were attacked. Masters and the military put 200 slaves to the sword and hunted down 400 more; they were tried, executed and had their bodies hanged at the plantation gates as a warning. Ministers of religion were blamed for agitation. The black ministers were executed, the whites imprisoned and deported, and all their churches were burned to the ground. [47]

The first news, sent via New York, did not reach England until February 1832. On the 23rd the *Newcastle Courant* published a report that included lurid reports from a Jamaican paper, also called the *Courant*. It gave 'particulars of an insurrection among the slaves' and announced that 'martial law had been proclaimed.'

[Slaves] had burnt a number of buildings ... an eminent lawyer, —Jackson of Old Harbour had been murdered in his house ... Ten o'clock. We have just received intelligence that the Palmyra Estate was extinguished after burning down one trash house' and 'understand the drivers on the neighbouring estates instead of going to their owners for orders as is usual, this being the last day of the holidays, have taken their matchets*, and have gone off, as they say, to their grounds. Eleven o'clock. The work of destruction is going on; the whole sky in the south west is illuminated ... From our office we see five distinct fires. Midnight. One fire is raging with unabated fury ... we apprehend it to be the whole of the works and buildings on the York Estate in this parish.

*large knives for cutting cane.

The *Newcastle Courant* also published a 'private' letter from the same source:

The troopers are flying around with dispatches ... Commerce is at a standstill ... the militia regiments are ready to act at a moment's notice. This promptitude ... it is to be hoped ... will have a salutary effect and prevent the effusion of blood; but for example's sake it is absolutely necessary that some shootings and hangings must take place. Bitter and fatal will be the discovery to be made by the poor deluded slaves when they become aware that no aid is to be expected ... from les amis de nègres, whose empty hypercritical babble, inflammatory writings and harangues have been the greatest incentives in urging them on to the desperate attempt on which they are engaged.

The reference to 'Negroes' friends' was probably a coded reference to the missionaries.

A letter in the following week's *Newcastle Courant* noted

That three Baptist Missionaries are in custody on a charge of having excited the slaves to rebellion. Their names were Wm Knibb, William Whitehorn, and Thos Abbott. The Jamaica journals ascribe this insurrection in a great measure to the sectarian preachers; but this will form a question for a future investigation. It is however to be feared that the zeal of those who are sent out, in too many instances exceeds their discretion.

John Fenwick, by then one of the town's leading abolitionists, complained that the editor had uncritically repeated the assertions of the partisan Jamaican authorities. He had worked with missionaries for many years and had never met one who could fit that description. One of the missionaries, William Knibb, wrote that he was 'wearied from trying to quell an insurrection in this parish.'[48] Similar sentiments were expressed by a leading London Baptist in *The Times*; he felt that preachers in Jamaica were quite rightly speaking of equality before God, and slaves may have interpreted that literally.

Northumberland Collections Service (SANT-BEQ-04-21-211a+b)

REV. WILLIAM KNIBB.
BORN 1803, DIED NOVEMBER 15, 1845.

William Knibb, who visited the North East after he left Jamaica.

The venomous charges against the missionaries, their persecution and the coarse violence of the Jamaican whites energised the anti-slavery movement in Britain. It focussed on immediate abolition, but the major question of parliamentary reform absorbed the Whig government's attention. The King had promised Grey that he would create enough peers to carry the day in the Lords if they refused to pass the Bill. In May the King went back on his promise. Grey resigned. There was an outburst of anger across the country that day. In Newcastle a requisition carrying 200 signatures demanded that the Mayor call a public meeting to protest. 40,000 were estimated to have turned out on the Spittal, carrying banners and hearing speeches from MPs. Almost all North East MPs supported reform. Similar mass meetings took place over the next few days in Darlington, Durham, Sunderland, Gateshead and Berwick. The message was clear. Reform was essential. Support for Grey was universal. The return of Wellington would be resisted. In the event, Wellington failed to form an administration, the King conceded defeat and Grey returned. In June the

Reform Bill went back to the Lords and it was passed.

North East abolitionists were amongst the staunchest supporters of the Reform Act, which delivered a fistful of new MPs who were mostly reformers. During the summer and into autumn there had been enormous mass meetings and celebratory dinners across the North East. Ten of thousands registered their enthusiasm in Darlington on June 9, Durham on the 20th, Newcastle and Sunderland on August 14, Newcastle again on August 24 Sunderland again on the 27th, Hexham on September 6, Gateshead on September 10, Newcastle yet again the following day and Alnwick on October 3. The Newcastle Society had tried to get North East parliamentary candidates to stand on an anti-slavery platform, but most of the favourites to win were already committed to abolition.[49]

Charles Earl Grey, author of the 1832 Reform Bill, by R. Hicks.

Riding on the anger raised by Jamaican reprisals and the enthusiasm for reform, Buxton tried to get a motion through the Commons calling for immediate abolition. He failed. The abolitionist movement was not appeased by Cabinet promises to put further pressure on colonial assemblies, because those assemblies were felt to be closed to discussion. In the event, several assemblies made scurrilous remarks about British politicians and some threatened to seek a political relationship with the United States.

The first General Election under the new electoral arrangements took place in December and January 1833. Reformers were swept to power, including 104 MPs pledged to abolition. The biggest loser was the West Indian interest. Its Commons membership was reduced by around 40 seats. However, the Reform Act did not alter the shape of the Lords. The government was committed to abolition, but afraid that an immediate declaration could risk insurrection in the colonies and the implacable hostility of the Lords, the King and the West India interest.

The months following the opening of Parliament were marked by an intense revival of anti-slavery campaigns. The Agency Committee's semi-professional organisers had been touring the country for more than a year, gaining support for immediate abolition. Its parent body, the London Anti-Slavery Society, grew rapidly and hundreds of local societies sprang up. During the year over 5,000 petitions were submitted with more than 1,000,000 signatures. The government, and especially one elected on the tide of broad sentiment for reform, could not ignore this.

In May '6,293 female inhabitants of Newcastle upon Tyne, Gateshead and their vicinities had signed the Ladies' Petition for the immediate abolition of Slavery.'[50] That month Buxton presented 800 women's petitions to Parliament and they were credited with helping to push the Whig cabinet to produce the Emancipation Bill that summer.[51] Some 300,000 women signed these petitions. 187,000 were from specifically female petitioning campaigns.[52]

The government took two months to prepare the Bill that it put before Parliament in May and it was another three months before it reached the statute book. The Bill was slightly amended and the Act received the royal assent on August 28. All slaves under the age of six were to be freed immediately. Slaves over the age of six

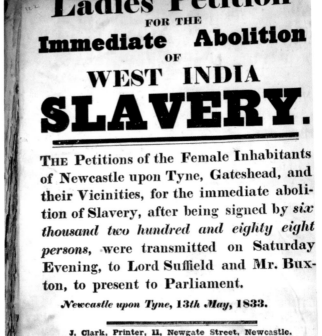

Ladies' Petition
FOR THE
Immediate Abolition
OF
WEST INDIA
SLAVERY.

THE Petitions of the Female Inhabitants of Newcastle upon Tyne, Gateshead, and their Vicinities, for the immediate abolition of Slavery, after being signed by *six thousand two hundred and eighty eight persons*, were transmitted on Saturday Evening, to Lord Suffield and Mr. Buxton, to present to Parliament.

Newcastle upon Tyne, 13th May, 1833.

J. Clark, Printer, 11, Newgate Street, Newcastle.

Tyne and Wear Archives DX17/1/122

were to remain as 'apprentices' for up to ten more years, but would have to be paid wages for the work they did in the quarter of the week when they were 'free'. The government would provide £20,000,000[53] – worth about £200 millions in 2008 – by way of compensation for slave-owners who lost their human property.[54] Slaves greeted the Act with ecstatic approval.

In summer Joseph Sturge, of Birmingham, argued that the strategy should be 'agitate, agitate, agitate. The people must emancipate the slaves for the Government never will.' He had no confidence in the terms of the Act and quickly turned his guns on the apprenticeship system. George Stephen shared his misgivings, declaring that the Agency Committee 'disowned compensation: it did more; it reprobated it as an indirect participation in the crime.'[55]

In Newcastle, 'rejoicings commenced' with 'a party of seventy persons partaking of an elegant cup of tea, in the vestry of New Court Chapel, and a public service in the New Road Wesleyan Chapel, which was completely filled by a deeply interested congregation.' Next day 'nearly 300 persons of various religious denominations, took tea together in the Music Hall, which was tastefully decorated with flowers and evergreens, and presented a very animated spectacle.' There were several speeches by local ministers and one by a guest speaker, the Leeds activist, George Carr. That evening they moved on to the Brunswick Chapel, 'crowded in every part'; it seated 800. The meeting, chaired by the schoolmaster, Mr Bruce, took several resolutions and heard a number of speeches including Mr Matthews, the former national secretary of the Anti-Slavery Society. The euphoric style of the event was underscored by 'a selection of appropriate hymns,' sung 'with considerable effect-particularly by Mr Montgomery, beginning, "Blow ye the trumpets abroad o'er the sea."'

At South Shields the celebrations were 'observed in a manner peculiarly interesting. In the morning the foundation stone of a large and commodious building intended for schools was laid.' At ten o'clock, a number of gentlemen sat down for an excellent breakfast at the Golden Lion. The meal was presided over by Dr Thomas Winterbottom, the veteran abolitionist who had served as medical officer to the ill-fated Sierra Leone colony from 1792-96. In the evening 'a union of seven congregations took place in the Primitive Methodists' Chapel, when a public thanksgiving was observed. The attendance was large.' At Darlington there was a stone laying for an

Independents' (Congregationalist) Sunday School, complete with speeches. Children connected with 'the schools of the Wesleyan Methodists assembled in a field near the town.' They heard an address and 'were treated with cakes.' There were also celebrations in Durham, Sunderland, North Shields and Berwick.

At the beginning of September readers of the *Newcastle Courant* received 'happy' news from Barbados. 'The first of August was observed, throughout the island, as a day of solemn thanksgiving. The Negroes attended their places of worship, and the day passed over in peace and harmony.' An anonymous letter published in the *Newcastle Courant* stated that 'never was Jamaica in a more contented and tranquil state than at this moment.' Many North Eastern abolitionists who adopted the radical Agency Committee's line had anxieties about the obscene amounts of compensation and the 'apprenticeship' system – more accurately, the postponement of genuinely free status – but they were largely suppressed in the joy of achievement.

EMANCIPATION FROM SLAVERY.—There is, we firmly believe, not one man in this vast empire who would have the hardihood to defend the "slave system" upon its "merits," who would deny that the blessing of freedom is the universal birthright of the human race, and that man, from his first entrance into the world, is, in the most unlimited sense of the term, FREE. But, as it has been quaintly, though forcibly expressed by Porson, "There are two descriptions of slavery, personal and mental;" and it has long been a disputed point amongst the learned disquisitionists which of the two is the most painful and humiliating. Leaving these disputants to settle the matter as they may, we will mention another description of slavery which partakes of the properties of both personal and mental—the slavery of pain and torture arising from that most excruciating disorder, the Gout. To those thus afflicted, and who desire to be speedily and effectually "emancipated," we advise them to have recourse to " BLAIR'S GOUT AND RHEUMATIC PILLS," in order that they may be put into possession of the enjoyment of " perfect freedom."—*Leeds Mercury*.

Newcastle Libraries

Jumping on the bandwagon. Newcastle Courant December 24, 1836, reproducing a letter in the Leeds Mercury, finds a topical way to advertise gout pills.

One can imagine the snort over a slave-owner's breakfast table at a newspaper report in January 1834: 'the planters are very anxious to receive the money awarded to them for the manumission of their slaves, and for the entire settlement of the affair.' In April 1835 a letter from Demerara recorded that, 'So far everything goes on well and far beyond the expectations of the most sanguine, so there is every prospect that the apprenticeship system would be found to give general satisfaction.' During 1836 Jamaican papers quoted in the *Newcastle Courant* mentioned that 'in the course of one year £34,000 has been raised by the Negroes to ransom 1000 of their body since the proclamation.'[56] Late in December a small item from a Demerara paper appeared in the *Newcastle Courant*:

> 'For sale, the services of the remainder of the apprenticeship of a valuable family of Negro People, apprentice labourers, comprising within itself all the requisite domestics for a small family, viz., Harriet, cook and washerwoman, aged 30; Marie, a lady's maid and seamstress, aged 14; Eliza, a house servant, aged 10 years; and Prins, a very active houseboy of 8 years. Apply, &—'

Apparently 'apprentices' were still regarded as property.[57]

MULTUM IN PARVO.—The following advertisement, taken from a Demerara paper, shows that the negroes have not lost all their value to their owners by the act of emancipation :— " For sale, the services of the remainder of the apprenticeship of a valuable family of N. P., apprenticed labourers, comprising within itself all the requisite domestics for a small family; viz., Harriet, a cook and washerwoman, aged 30 ; Maria, a lady's maid and sempstress, aged 14 ; Eliza, a house servant, aged 10 years ; and Prins, a very active house-boy of eight years. Apply", &c.—400l. have now been subscribed at Leicester, for erecting a monument to Wicliffe. The sum required

Newcastle Libraries

8 Fighting the terms of the Act

After the Emancipation Act of 1834 people quickly became aware of the implications of two attached conditions; the apprenticeship system and the generous compensation granted to slave holders for the loss of their property. Although it was accepted that little could be done about the latter, fierce opposition developed to the former.

By early 1836 The London Anti-Slavery Society had resurfaced with a new name: The Society for Abolishing Slavery all over the World. George Thompson, one of Britain's leading and most vociferous abolitionists, had recently returned from a controversial speaking tour in the United States, where he had faced verbal and physical abuse. The transatlantic connection became a key part of his strategy.[58]

On March 31, Thompson spoke at the first meeting of the renamed Newcastle upon Tyne Society for Abolishing Slavery all over the World in Brunswick Place Chapel. The new Society appointed new officers, condemned slavery in the United States, a fact 'revolting to the Declaration of Independence's claim, "that all men are created equal,"' and agreed to correspond with US abolitionists. Newcastle abolitionists fell under the influence of the more radical wing of the movement led by Thompson as well as George Stephen and the young Darlington Quaker, Elizabeth Pease, who worked closely with Thompson to develop the transatlantic link. They wanted to encourage the full participation of women in the anti-slavery mission.

Brunswick Methodist Church, Newcastle

Brunswick Methodist Chapel, built 1820.

Thompson was in Newcastle again in April, probably with Elizabeth Pease. He addressed 'a very numerous assembly of ladies' in the Friends' Meeting House in Pilgrim Street. In a lecture that lasted an hour and a half, 'he entered fully into the state of slavery and the slave trade throughout the world,' and ended by pointing out the ways 'in which a Ladies' Society might assist in the great work of universal abolition' He 'urged the formation of a society, and the vigorous prosecution of the benevolent prize in concert with kindred institutions in this country, and on the other side of the

Private Collection; scanned by Northumberland Collections Service

Elizabeth Pease.

Atlantic.'[59] A Ladies' Emancipation Society was founded at the end of the meeting. There were a number of volunteers to collect money and distribute Tracts. (In December they sent an address to Boston.)

Thompson became a frequent visitor to Newcastle and other North East towns. In January 1837 he visited the new Salem Chapel in Hood Street, Newcastle, one of the elegant new streets in the ambitious Dobson-Grainger development in the town centre. (The new Theatre Royal would open nearby in February.) The meeting was packed out and his address, which lasted for almost two hours, was punctuated by laughter and applause. It was reported in full in the local papers. He was clearly a remarkable speaker, yet it was a deeply serious speech. He subjected the 'apprenticeship' system to precise analysis, laced with ridicule. He spared no one, including the parliamentary drafters of the Bill; Lord Stanley, the

Minister who introduced it; the MPs who voted for it to become an Act; and the special magistrates, 'smoke dried planters' and overseers who administered it. The audience was shocked by his descriptions of the treatment of Africans, including a description of a woman held in a neck collar and literally flogged to death. The rapid end of the system was his immediate goal, but he warned that white society in the colonies was so base that the anti-slavery movement would need to continue and to strengthen itself, even after the present situation had been remedied.

George Thompson.

During 1837 evidence of abuse of the 'apprenticeship' system mounted. In November a delegation of over 30 MPs, including the North Easterners Sir Matthew White Ridley, Christopher Blackett and William Ord, walked to Downing Street to meet the Prime Minister, Lord Melbourne. They tried to persuade him to end the system and suspend compensation payments. They had a mountain of evidence, but Melbourne brushed it, and them, aside with a vague promise of getting the Colonial Office to raise the issues. The delegates were further dismayed when their chief spokesman, Buxton, · suggested that further parliamentary activity might be counter-productive.

The movement stepped up its activity in a flurry of petitioning, including a vast Ladies' Society petition to the new Queen Victoria. Melbourne advised her to ignore it, and she did. The Newcastle society heard two well-attended lectures by Thompson and members would have read a long letter from John Scoble in the *Newcastle Courant* about the national Society setting out the Special Magistrates' punishments under the 'apprenticeship' system. The paper also contained a précis of a speech in Jamaica by the Governor, Lord Sligo, who charged the Assembly with completely ignoring his directions on carrying out the Colonial Office's instructions on punishments (flogging of females), gaol conditions, taxation of the property of 'apprentices' and their education.[60]

In March 1838 another attempt to get Parliament to end the 'apprenticeship' system was defeated, largely because some of the formerly abolitionist MPs took the Melbourne position that the system would come to an end in two to four years and that it was advisable to maintain stability and avoid the risk of 'exciting' the Negroes and angering the planters. The Newcastle delegates to a London conference preceding the debate in Parliament reported back to a large meeting at Brunswick Place Chapel. After hissing backsliding by local MPs, the meeting decided to pressurise them and to petition Parliament.

In June came truly surprising news. The Jamaican Assembly had decided to end the 'apprenticeship' system on August 1, because they had reached the end of their patience with the continued protests from Britain, inside and outside of Parliament. It later became clear that the system itself was damaging production. Moreover, despite brutal punishments, including the installation of treadmills, black people did not co-operate with masters. Other colonies followed suit.

At midnight on July 31 William Knibb spoke in his Jamaican chapel and the congregation 'simultaneously rose, and broke into a loud and continued burst of exaltation.' He wrote to a friend:

> Never did I hear such a sound. The winds of freedom appeared to have been let loose. The very building shook at the strange yet sacred joy.

Next day Knibb conducted a ceremony burying a coffin:

> containing the instruments of slavery, a whip, a chain, and an iron collar ... while the congregation sang a mock dirge. "Now, slavery we lay thy vile form

Newcastle Libraries (Anti-slavery Tracts vol I)

An interior view of a Jamaican house of correction. This barbaric punishment, inflicted on men and women, young and old, involved hanging from a bar above the wheel to 'dance the step' with the feet. People who could not 'dance the step' would be badly cut on the legs as the wheel turned (fast or slow according to the whim of the supervisor), and were also flogged. Some estate owners were blatant about their intentions to weaken apprentices before their time was served out. (From 'Narrative by James Williams', an escaped slave who arrived in England in the mid-1830s.)

in the dust ..." ... The flag of freedom, with the union-jack at the corner of it, was hoisted amid cheers.

It was a day of intense and unqualified jubilation across the island:

> As at the abolition four years previously the black people behaved admirably, celebrating the great day in a spirit of innocent rejoicing which gladdened the hearts of their well-wishers ... It was more like a religious festival. The chapels everywhere were filled with worshippers giving thanks. In Spanish Town there were great crowds in the Square in front of King's House, with Sir Lionel [Smith] making a speech amid much affectionate cheering: processions of chanting, banner-waving children, and happy crowds again at the Baptist chapel, where the Minister, Mr Phillippo, was hoisted shoulder-high and carried in triumph into his house. On some of the estates there

were dinners where three or four hundred people sat down together, labourers and employers and ministers of religion with their families, at long tables under arbours of coconut branches decked with flowers and flags; for the moment a sweet temper prevailed, loyal toasts were drunk and the planters congratulated the people on their freedom ...[61]

On August 1 the Newcastle Society met at Salem Chapel. Reportedly, participants were well aware that they faced very great tasks. They passed a motion thanking God, before moving onto secular matters. They thanked Lord Brougham, Joseph Sturge, John Scoble and George Thompson, perhaps pointedly omitting the local man, Earl Grey and local MPs, whom they believed to be guilty of backsliding. It was a real Thompson flourish, immediately after the triumph, to agree 'to the Use of all lawful Means within its power, until the black and coloured races of our West India Colonies are placed on an Equality as to all Civil Rights with the rest of the Inhabitants.' They also touched on bringing an end to the slave trade internationally and on the contracting of 'the hill coolies' of India to work in Guiana, for which they firmly blamed the government. The meeting could not end 'without tendering its hearty congratulations to the venerable

Thomas Clarkson whose life has been mercifully spared to witness a Triumph of the great Principles of Justice and Humanity, which he was among the first to advocate and enforce'.[62] This motion was moved by the North East's own venerable pioneer of abolition, the Reverend William Turner, still active in his 78th year.

The Newcastle Ladies' Emancipation Society met later in August 'to take into consideration a request from the Gentlemen's Committee. It was resolved to accede to it & immediately to

Thomas Clarkson.

Newcastle Libraries (Collard & Ross)

Grey Street and the Theatre Royal in about 1841, the Turk's Head was close by, as was Hood Street. The monument to Earl Grey was erected in 1838.

commence making the needful arrangements for a tea-party to be held tomorrow in the Turks Head Long Room to commemorate the liberation of the Apprentices in the West Indies Colonies.'[63] For many in Newcastle the ending of apprenticeship must have brought a sense of closure; for the most senior among them it was the successful culmination of the battle stretching right back to the last decades of the previous century. The remaining issues were so much more daunting. They included the ending of slave trading on a world scale, the correction of abuses in the British Empire including the province of the mighty East India Company and the biggest beast of all, slavery in the American South. They would take at least another 50 years of organised agitation. The British movement would go through many troughs when it could be reduced to a tiny number of relentless enthusiasts. This would be true of the North East of England but there would be flurries of larger scale involvement, firstly perhaps as a spin off from the great movement of the 1830s and then around the American Civil War in the early 1860s.

9 The Distinguished Advocate ...

After apprenticeship was summarily ended in 1838 attention moved to world-wide slavery. The subject provoked much tactical debate. It brought British and American anti-slavery activists closer together. There were several tours of former slaves to the North East.

After 1838 the anti slavery movement had to struggle to keep in the public eye. It was not only because its goals were less focussed. The 1830s and 1840s were turbulent decades. Just weeks before the Salem Chapel meeting in July 1838 the young Queen Victoria had been crowned. The Newcastle elite planned great celebrations but the town's rebellious elements resolved to disrupt them. Today the monarchy is usually regarded with warm affection at best and moderately satirical tolerance at worst. This was not so in the century before 1850. In the weeks leading up to the Coronation the radicals were printing attacks on the process including the cost, citing the bill of £248,000 for the coronation of the 'scandalous' George IV in 1821.

On Coronation Day, June 23, a mass protest meeting took place on the Town Moor addressed by Feargus O'Connor, the leading Chartist, among others. The Hussars and two companies of Foot marched and countermarched around the gathering with bayonets fixed. This evoked memories of Peterloo and became an issue with which radicals could beat the authorities around the head in the months ahead. This was just the *hors d'oeuvres* because 1838-1839 was the moment for Chartism to rise and Newcastle was one of the epicentres of its first phase. The reformist alliance of 1832-3, brought together in the Northern Political Union, was split into moderate and revolutionary wings. This is another story, but when 40,000 men and women could march across the region to meet on the Town Moor, on Christmas Day 1838, demanding universal suffrage, a period of considerable turmoil is indicated.[64]

Debate was very sharp and old friends fell out. A good example was Dr John Fife, long-term abolitionist and former Chairman of the Northern Political Union. He had been a member of the town council since the elections of 1836. These were the first municipal elections following the Municipal Corporations Act of 1835 which had destroyed the old Corporation. In November 1839 Fife was elected Mayor and the former poacher became the game-keeper, riding forth to put down a Chartist riot. A meeting of the Northern Political Union declined to include him in their committee, demanding an explanation for his conduct. Fife had been preceded as Mayor by Dr Headlam, another member of the Political Union who, like Fife was an ardent abolitionist. He favoured immediate universal suffrage.

The abolitionists usually steered clear of political issues unless they clearly affected the slavery question, but the lively people who made up the mass support for anti-slavery would have strong opinions on the biggest questions of the day, suffrage extension and secret ballots. Nationally, Lord John Russell supported each of the abolition measures and was an architect of the 1832 Reform Act, but he argued that the Act had achieved perfection for the British Constitution. Joseph Sturge, perhaps the leading national figure in 1830s anti-slavery activity, disagreed with Russell and argued for household suffrage. George Thompson disagreed with Russell and Sturge, and argued for universal suffrage. He became the MP for Tower Hamlets in 1847 on the Chartist ticket.[65] These differences ran through the constituency which formed the mass movement for abolition of slavery and nowhere more so than in the North East.

Earl Grey was responsible for both the Reform Bill and the Emancipation Act of 1833. For him there might be future reform but at some distant date. He positively disapproved of popular initiatives. The North East movements on both issues fell on the radical side. The Northern Political Union was very hostile to the Reform Act's limitations. It quickly moved onto the offensive after the Act was passed. Likewise, local abolitionists adopted the line of the radical Agency Committee, being deeply aggrieved by the negative aspects of the Emancipation Act, namely 'apprenticeship' and compensation. Of the locals, Thomas Doubleday,[66] Unitarian soap manufacturer, supported universal suffrage and the immediate abolition of slavery.

The most popular anti-slavery speaker in the North East was George Thompson. The frequency of his visits suggests he saw the area as fertile ground for pushing ahead the provincial campaign. It was not just

Newcastle. Sunderland, too, shared an enthusiasm for his attention and he also became close to the Pease family of Darlington. He was particularly admired by Elizabeth Pease who, unusually for a Quaker, had strong views on the suffrage question, including support for the Chartists. For this she attracted the disapproval of fellow Quakers. Thompson was a strong advocate of independent female activity and, with Pease, helped to create and build the Ladies' Groups. Anna Richardson of Newcastle was closely involved, but we have no evidence of her public interest in the suffrage question.

The radical democrats (Chartists) strongly supported the steps towards the abolition of slavery and were active at some level. However they were sharply critical of those mainstream anti-slavery propagandists who gave little or no attention to the serious oppression of British working people beyond supporting the provision of soup kitchens. Joseph Pease, life long anti-slavery activist, and, from 1834, MP for South Durham, was severely criticised by Doubleday and friends for supporting the New Poor Law. Members of the Political Union saw it as introducing prisons (work houses) for the poor.

Tyne and Wear Museums

This knitted pincushion bears the emblem of the abolitionists, the 'supplicant slave' as seen on coins, medals, and tracts.

All of these tensions were felt as the Anti-Slavery movement moved beyond the end of 'apprenticeship' in the summer of 1838. Despite such divisions, and the sense of victory in 1838, the abolitionists did not see the job as done. George Thompson was back in town in February 1839. He gave one of his mammoth talks at the Primitive Methodist Chapel in Nelson Street, only five minutes walk from the Salem and Brunswick chapels. He was there to promote his new campaign, the Aborigines' Protection Society. From the Chairman, John Fife's, account, it was a crowded meeting. Fife opened it with a strong statement:

> It was a melancholy and almost incredible fact, that, although our government boasted in the name of Christian, wherever the British flag waved over our colonies, it had been the emblem, not so much of peace, not so much of happiness, as of misery and desolation. It might be said as Shakespeare said of Coriolanus, to have gone forth with noise before and with tears behind.

Thompson followed, giving a detailed account of the history of the British Empire. He touched upon the Caribbean, Africa and Tasmania before focussing upon the dismal situation in India. There was rhetoric in his lectures. He was an audience pleaser but even 170 years later his impact is clear. Here is a small extract on famine:

> Within the past 12 months, in one part of India, half a million had perished prematurely. And why? Was the land sterile? It was the garden and granary of the world. Were the people barbarous? They were as easily teachable, as industrious and capable as ourselves. Was there no corn in the country? Yes, the granaries teemed with the products of the land, but-they were under lock and key, and bayonets surrounded the doors, to drive the hungry wretch to perish on the road. Now hunger was said to be a sharp thorn; and the first thing they must do was to give the people bread. It was useless, in the first instance, offering them anything else. To offer religion to a starving multitude was to mock them. Their answer was, perish your religion, give us bread …[67]

He went on this vein, speaking in short, sharp, unembroidered sentences. His audience must have gone away moved and informed by lucid argument.

In the previous month of January, the *Newcastle Chronicle* carried an appeal headed 'Testimonial to George Thompson, Esq., The Distinguished Advocate of Universal Emancipation'. It had originated in Glasgow where 700 people had subscribed. Newcastle and its locality were invited to join the appeal which was designed to create a salary for Thompson as a full-time organiser. £60 was quickly subscribed on a list which included Sarah Beaumont, of the Ladies' Group; Mr Jonathan Priestman and Mrs Anna Richardson, well known Quakers; several of the Committee members of the Anti-Slavery Society; and oddly, Joseph Lamb, town councillor and partner of the plantation-owning Graham Clarkes.[68]

The Societies of Newcastle, South Shields, Sunderland and Darlington sent delegates to the first international Anti-Slavery Convention held in London in the summer of 1840. This was an extraordinary meeting that debated procedure as much as content. The largest international contingent was the American one. It included a majority of women. This was unacceptable to most British delegates. They refused to have the American women sit in the body of the conference though a minority, including George Thompson, favoured accepting the American delegation as presented. The result was that, after interminable wrangling, the women agreed to sit in the gallery so that the conference could proceed. The American leader, William Lloyd Garrison was delayed at Liverpool and missed the procedural debate. On arrival he attempted to reopen the discussion but was denied, and in an act of solidarity joined the women in the gallery, which did no harm at all to his reputation with many female abolitionists. Maria Waring said: 'William Lloyd Garrison is one of God's nobility ... I don't think I ever saw such an angelic holy looking face.'[69]

The major issues at the Conference concerned US slavery, the ongoing slave trade practised by Spain, Portugal and 'independent' French and Americans, slave grown produce, indentured Indian labour and the situation in British India. It was clear that there was a very large mountain to climb.

Opposite, The Anti-Slavery Convention, 1840, by Benjamin Robert Haydon. Oil on canvas, 1841. On the very far right edge, with red hair, is Elizabeth Pease. Thomas Clarkson is speaking. George Thompson is 4th from the right, front row. John Scoble is seated with his back to us on the right. William Knibb is just to his left. Jonathan Backhouse is to Clarkson's left behind the lady in the bonnet.
(National Portrait Gallery, London).

Shortly after the Conference ended, the Newcastle Society met twice in a week to consider its findings and to determine what they might do.

The perceived importance of Newcastle is suggested by the speakers who attended the meetings and moved resolutions. They included J.G. Birney of New York, a future US Presidential Candidate; Henry Stanton, Secretary of the American Anti-Slavery Society; and John Scoble of the national Anti-Slavery Society. The American connection was to be sustained over the following years as

Sir H.H. Johnson, 'The Negro in the New World', 1910

William Lloyd Garrison pictured in later life.

Garrison, Frederick Douglass and William Wells Brown were to make visits to promote their campaigns to end slavery in the Southern States of their country. It was a two-way process because eventually George Thompson would be a popular figure on the other side of the Atlantic and Elizabeth Pease would cultivate a strong alliance with the American sisters.

The Newcastle meetings discussed further organisational changes including taking responsibility for drawing the various regional societies together. Despite this, there are no records of further meetings of the Society in the area for the next seven years. This could mean that there were none or that they were too insignificant for the press to take note. The only other events of the Anti-Slavery Society that we know about took place on January 1 and 2, 1847 when, 'Members and friends of the Anti-Slavery League held a soirée in the Music Hall (Nelson Street), when about 700 people sat down to tea.' Jonathan Priestman chaired the proceedings. The audience enthusiastically welcomed Frederick Douglass, 'the fugitive slave,' Henry Wright, the American friend of William Lloyd Garrison, and Mr Smith, secretary of the national Anti-Slavery society.[70] Characteristically, given the divided nature of the movement after 1838, both meetings appear to have been largely concerned with differences of opinion within the movement. What the large Newcastle audience thought of the discussion of the attitude of some Christian churches in Britain to some Christian churches in America or an alleged attack on Garrison in an American paper is not recorded! It all seems to confirm what is known of the declining years of the campaign which had enjoyed such success in the previous decade.

During this period there were two broad tendencies in the anti-slavery movement. After the World Conference of 1840, the minority round William Lloyd Garrison promoted passive resistance through mass involvement. His supporters became predominant in the diminishing movement. As the focus on parliamentary action became less relevant, the old guard like Thomas Fowell Buxton lost their grip. His status was already in doubt because of the total failure of his ambitious scheme to create a utopia for freed slaves on the banks of the Niger. Parliamentary efforts to eradicate the slave trade had also flagged, partly due to diminishing enthusiasm for deploying the Royal Navy at great expense. The more insistent question was the strength of slavery in the American south about which parliament could do nothing.

American abolitionists had long been interested in the British situation. Friendships already existed across the Atlantic. This was deepened by the events at the World Conference. The Garrison strategy appealed to Quakers and the North East was a region where the Friends were strong. Garrison was close to George Thompson and, whilst neither were Friends, they were close to Joseph and Elizabeth Pease. Darlington was on the road to Edinburgh and Glasgow, both bastions of Garrisonian ideas and Thompson often

Frederick Douglass (1817-1895), was the son of a plantation owner and a slave. Born in Maryland, he escaped in 1838 and became a lecturer with the American Anti-Slavery Society.

85

stopped off at the Pease home at Feethams. Elizabeth Pease became a strong supporter. She wrote pamphlets, which was very unusual for a woman at that time. She openly corresponded with American abolitionists and helped to build women's anti-slavery organisations across the country. She even travelled with Thompson as a secretary, an enormous risk to her reputation. All this was true of the 1840s but by the early 1850s she had broadened the number of issues in which she was involved. In 1852 she married John Pringle Nichol, a Glasgow professor of astronomy, and left the North East.[71]

Encouraging abstention from the products of slavery was an objective as old as the anti-slavery movement itself. It was thought to be an activity especially appropriate for women supporters because its focus was the domestic economy over which women were thought to rule. Even this was too much for some male activists, like William Wilberforce, who wished to draw the line at door-to-door canvassing for support. In the 1790s early campaigners had tried to promote a boycott of slave-grown sugar in which Newcastle people played some part. Several individuals, male and female, continued their abstention for life, but the public campaigns involving lots of people were episodic and brief. This was true of the second sugar boycott, organised in response to the Anti-Slavery Society's acceptance, in 1824, of Prime Minister George Canning's promise to put pressure on the planters to improve slave conditions. The campaigners wanted immediate abolition so organised a boycott of slave-grown sugar in an attempt to damage the planters' profits. By the 1830s the boycott was effectively swept up into general activity for emancipation.

The next initiative was taken in the late 1840s with the Newcastle

William Wells Brown (1814-1884), whose visit to South Shields is advertised opposite, was an escaped slave with a white father, plantation owner George Higgins. He was one of seven children, all with different fathers. William took the name of his friend Wells Brown, a Quaker, who helped him obtain freedom. He eventually became a lecturing agent for the New York Anti-Slavery Society, wrote several books, and made a living from lecturing.

W. Wells Brown, 'Three Years in Europe', 1852

CENTRAL HALL,
SOUTH SHIELDS.

FRONT SEATS, 6D.
BACK SEATS, 3D.

On Wednesday Evening the 15th, and Thursday Evening the 16th February,

Doors open at Half-past Seven, LECTURE to Commence at Eight o'clock.

Hunting the Slave with the Negro Dogs.

Death of the President's Daughter.

W. WELLS BROWN,

A Fugitive Slave from the United States (Author of " Clotel, or the President's Daughter ;" "Three Years in Europe " &c.), will Lecture on American Slavery. The subject will be illustrated by new and splendid Dissolving Views, painted expressly for the purpose.

The following, with other Scenes, will be brought before the Audience.

SCENES ON THE COAST OF AFRICA.
The Slave Ship, Branding of Slaves.
Chase of a Slaver by an English Man-of-war
SLAVE MARKET.
THE HEROIC WOMAN.
THE ATTEMPT TO ESCAPE ; THE ARREST.
Chasing of Fugitives with Negro Dogs.
STAKING AND THE BASTINADO.
INTERIOR OF UNCLE TOM'S CABIN AT NIGHT.
The Slave-trader & his Victim. The Anxious Mother.
THE TRADER THROWN FROM HIS HORSE—
JOLIFICATION.
ELIZA CROSSING THE RIVER ON THE ICE.
The Mother and her Child in the Forest.
Curious Scene, all sorts of People.
The Broad Brim; the Negro's Friend.
THE MOUNTAIN PASS ; THE TERRIFIC FALL.
The President's Mansion at Washington.
CAPITOL OF THE UNITED STATES.
Mississippi River, Gorgeous Scenery.
THE FLOATING PALACE. THE BURNING BOAT.
The Mother's Escape. Rescue of Eva by Uncle Tom.
TOPSY & EVA. DEATH OF EVA.

The elderly young lady and the servant girl.
Simon Legree and his Gang of Slaves.
THE BLACK DRIVERS AND THEIR VICTIM.
DEATH OF UNCLE TOM.
A Wonderful Escape. The Negro Dogs.
The Red Indian and the Fugitive Slave in the Burning Prarie.
Wm. Wells Brown Caught by Negro Dogs.
THE HAPPY FAMILY BROKEN UP.
Escape of W. Wells Brown & his Mother.
THE YOUNG SLAVE IN THE ROCKING CHAIR
A New Mode of Obtaining an Education.
Successful Escape of William Wells Brown.
A FUGITIVE AT THE FALLS OF NIAGARA.
THE ESCAPE THROUGH DISGUISE.
A Slave Family in the Forest Worshiping God.
The English Shore.
Meeting of Fugitives in the land of Freedom.
Slaves protected by the British Flag.
The California Gold Fields.
SLAVES AT THE DIGGINGS.

Quakers in the forefront. This was the Free Produce Movement. Among its main campaigners were the Newcastle Quakers Anna Richardson, her husband Henry and his sister Ellen, who were to be among the area's most enthusiastic supporters for 60 years. They worked closely with their American sisters in the same kind of campaign. They revived the defunct Newcastle Ladies' Emancipation Society and financially supported an organiser, a black American abolitionist, Henry Highland Garnett. In the years between 1846 and 1854 they managed to found

Quaker activist, Anna Richardson.

Newcastle Literary and Philosophical Society

25 groups, 13 of which were in the North East.[72] By the 1840s, and especially in relation to US slavery, the principal product under attack was cotton. Britain was one of the main markets for American cotton and the campaigners felt they could make a real impact. Garnett's brief was to take the argument round meetings.

Like all consumer-based campaigns it faced serious problems. Sourcing an alternative commodity at a price and quality that people would buy was pretty well insurmountable. Even denting what was one of Britain's biggest import/export industries was a task which would need hundreds of thousands of supporters and almost certainly hundreds of working-class, as well as middle-class, organisers. It was also very dependent on the good health and energy of the small band of enthusiasts. It was largely a women's initiative but in the male-dominated society of Victorian England any public female activity provoked enormous hostility.

II

Connections

The movement for abolition tells the story of slavery from the point of view of those who opposed it and were prepared to devote hours of their lives to register their disgust with the system in general. Local connections with the slavery business have hardly played any part in that story. To leave it there would be interesting but very misleading. What is missing are the hidden chains which ran all the way from slave ship and plantation into the region linking them to rich and powerful families, adventurers, refugees from oppression, clergymen, soldiers and common seamen. Part Two of this story explores their side of the story and looks at how silence and politeness enabled them to live and socialise alongside abolitionists.

Newcastle around 1779.

10 The North East they left behind

The North East was a very troubled region during the 17th and early 18th centuries. Its families were continuously caught up in religious and civil strife. However the economy was undergoing rapid, if uneven, change. Many people reaped great rewards but there were victims too.

From the mid-16th century the coal economy in the Tyne Valley and to the south and west of Newcastle grew dramatically, largely because of the London market. In 1600 Queen Elizabeth granted the Newcastle Merchant Adventurers' Company[73] a monopoly of the North East coast coal trade, in return for 6d tax per chaldron.[74] Exports from the Tyne rose from 35,000 tons in 1565 to 400,000 tons in 1625. Dozens, if not hundreds, of tiny coal pits were sunk freely on the north bank of the river and, with the monarch's permission, on the south bank too; but throughout the 17th and 18th centuries the London market remained in the vice-like grip of around ten Merchant Adventurers known as 'hostmen'.[75]

Merchants had been the controlling elite in the most populous areas of the North East since the misty middle ages. Powerful families such as the Carrs, Ellisons, Liddells, Burdons, Cotesworths, Ridleys, Riddells, Scotts, Burdons, Blacketts, Ords, Ordes, Cramlingtons and Surtees' controlled trade, industry, social and civic life. By 1700 they had overtaken many of the older gentry families. During the 18th century prosperity and growth created the first consumer boom and some of the wealthiest North East merchants acquired or built grand houses.

Economic development in the North East was still constrained by political realities. There were winners and losers in the Civil War in the early 1660s, after the 'Glorious Revolution'[76] in 1689, the first Jacobite Rebellion of 1715 and the second in 1745. The close proximity of the Scottish border, at a time when Scots were seeking to settle accounts with their rulers in London, meant that North Easterners were repeatedly compelled to choose sides and this had a destabilising effect.

During the 18th century Newcastle's population grew from possibly under 20,000 in 1700 by around 10 per cent each decade, mainly because of

Newcastle Libraries (local colour prints)

Newcastle Guildhall in 1786.

the booming coal trade, and the town became well established as a regional capital. Townspeople were used to welcoming strangers. Drovers brought herds and flocks from Cumberland and the borders. Many people from the rural areas of northern England and southern Scotland settled in the town. They had been driven out of their homes by agricultural enclosure which allowed the gentry to take possession of the common land where poorer people had previously kept their livestock.

Foreign tongues and accents would be commonplace in the town. Shipping lists, published in Newcastle papers in 1776, showed arrivals and departures to and from London, Leith (for Edinburgh), Aberdeen, Riga, Copenhagen, Memel, Hamburg, Bremen, the Scheldt, Le Havre, Bordeaux, Cadiz, Oporto, Philadelphia, Boston, New York, Charleston, Jamaica and Barbados.[77] Seamen, those 'citizens of the world', teemed onto Newcastle's quayside, bringing goods, news and tall tales. Some made it their home port. Some settled. Scandinavian, Baltic, German, Dutch, Irish, French and

Italian surnames in parish registers show just what a cosmopolitan place Tyneside was. Of 460 men from HMS *Newcastle*, a Royal Navy frigate that visited the Tyne in 1816, 30 per cent of the crew had been born in Ireland, 30 per cent were from the port towns of southern England, 30 per cent were from the rest of England (including Tyneside), Wales and Scotland, and 10 per cent from Continental Europe, Africa, North America and the Caribbean.[78]

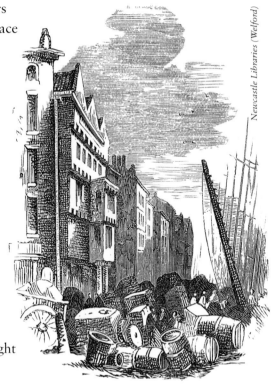

Newcastle Libraries (Welford)

The road journey to London from Newcastle took 36 arduous hours, but the daily coaches brought lawyers, merchants of all stripes, bankers, book-sellers, preachers, pamphleteers and musicians. The single most important factor in all this traffic was the expanding demand for coal. Great fortunes were made at both ends of the sea passage from the Tyne to the Thames. Tyneside merchants and their agents were regular visitors to London and mingled with international traders at the exchange, the coffee houses and, in season, the assemblies. Coal also went to France, the Low Countries, the Baltic, Russia and even across the Atlantic.

Developments along Northumberland Street and fashionable Westgate Street created up-market suburbs and the new money helped to build and furnish the Assembly Rooms, where assemblies, balls and concerts aimed to rival those in Bath, Brighton and even London.

To the west of the Guildhall, on the Close there

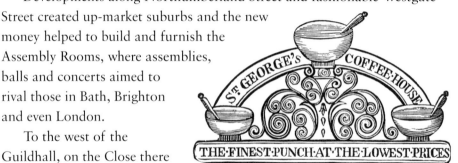

S.T. GEORGE'S COFFEE-HOUSE

THE·FINEST·PUNCH·AT·THE·LOWEST·PRICES

Tyne and Wear Museums

This genteel tea set dates from around 1780. The decoration features a black page boy. Initially tea was fairly expensive, but soon passed down the social scale.

was a complex of warehouses and factories, among them a sugar house. Opposite the Guildhall on Sandhill was Katy's Coffee House, established in the early 1800s. There were three coffee houses on Sandhill and two in other parts of the town, informal business centres where deals could be struck and settled on the shake of a hand. Local and national newspapers could be read and opinions exchanged about issues of the day. On the menu would be tobacco, coffee, tea, cocoa and, in Newcastle, rum – the essential ingredient of punch. Each of these commodities had their origins thousands of miles away in the Caribbean, North America or the Far East. The drinks are bitter so the final commodity, sugar, was a welcome addition.

Side was the main route from the Quayside to the upper part of town, lined with shops and dwelling houses. Including Sandgate, there were nearly 100 premises between the water side and St Nicholas' church at the top of the hill – grocers, milliners, tea dealers, tobacco merchants, wine merchants, goldsmiths, drapers, shoemakers, bakers. Around the churchyard there were grocers and tea merchants, a music teacher, a dancing master, a school, a bookseller (one of 11 in town), Thomas Bewick's printing workshop and the free Thomlinson Library attached to the church. A consumer society was in the making.

In the street by the church would be found the carriers who took goods from Newcastle across the North East and west to Carlisle, Cockermouth and Whitehaven, the slave trading port. Early directories show that each week over 40 wagons set off. The grocers of Morpeth, Alnwick, Hexham, North Shields, South Shields, Durham and Cumbria got their coffee, tea, sugar, pots and metal goods, books and newspapers and letters from the carriers. The London-Edinburgh coach would pass by too. The town was buzzing with commercial and social activity.

Tyne and Wear Museums

Rum decanter, made in Bristol, around 1800.

11 White settlers, free and unfree

People from the middle and lower orders of society made their way to the New World. In the case of prisoners they had no choice, transportation being the welcome alternative to hanging. Others, perhaps down on their luck, chose indentured service. At least at the end of the agreed period they were free to make their own way in the new country.

In December 1729 Newcastle watchmaker William Moralee arrived in Philadelphia. He later wrote:

> The Condition of bought servants is very hard, notwithstanding their indentures are made in England … I sold my red coat for a Quart of Rum, my Tie Wig for Sixpence, with which I bought a Threepenny Loaf, and a Quart of Cyder. Our Cargo consisted of Voluntary slaves, who are the least to be pitied. I saw all my Companions sold off before me; my turn came last, when I was sold for eleven pounds, to one Mr Isaac Pearson … I attempted an Escape, but was taken and put into prison.[79]

Moralee had fallen on hard times. When seeking work in London he had met an indenturing agent at an Inn in London. He accepted the man's terms, a free passage to America in return for three years servitude. Because of labour shortages in the New World, entrepreneurs imported ship loads of white people to do skilled work and some of the domestic work.

In 1775 the *Georgia Pacquet* stood on Newcastle Quayside for a month. Its captain advertised in the *Newcastle Chronicle* of August 7 for indentured servants to spend three years in North America.

> The Georgia Pacquet, bound for Savannah. The back settlements of Georgia are universally allowed by all authors to enjoy a perpetual spring and the most agreeable temperature of climate as well as to produce with the least trouble the most valuable products of the world … the greatest encouragement is given for indentured servants to go out … who after their time of service is expired will be enabled to settle on this land as proprietors … The province of Georgia is in no way concerned in the present disputes with this country.

The revolt of the North American colonies that was to end in the War of Independence was underway. Indentured service was presented as something of a holiday with a wonderful bonus at the end, but an indentured servant became the property of his or her master to be used at will. There were severe punishments for recalcitrant behaviour. The ship's manifest lists the people who arrived in Savannah in September 1775 to be sold into service. They were not Newcastle's poorest folk, but were mainly young people with skills: carpenters, wheelwrights, clerks, watchmakers, plasterers, bakers and male and female servants.[80] They could be bound for up to seven years before they would be free. In Georgia they would work in a plantation economy. Many would become attached to the plantation system as overseers or drivers with direct power over black slaves' lives. Even those in the south who never worked in plantations would be likely serve that system and support its practices.

The English courts also played a part in helping to solve the labour problem. From the early 18th century, transportation to the new American colonies became a deliberate public policy. Tyneside felons could be carried to London for transportation but ships did leave the Tyne directly bound for Virginia. Jonathan Blagdon, the business associate of sometime Mayor, William Cramlington, made a business out of this activity from the mid-18th century.[81] Although almost any labour input was welcome to farmers and planters they could be very cautious about employing felons who might be dangerous to life and property.[82]

William Marr, the son of a Morpeth blacksmith, went to Carolina in 1721 at the age of 28. Marr's will and inventory suggest that he may have taken sizeable funds because he founded a highly successful tanning business and acquired a sugar plantation. In a letter home he suggested that another Morpeth individual contemplating emigration to Carolina would need about £100 to make a satisfactory start. This was a very substantial sum of money, worth around £100,000 at today's values. His letters give a strong hint that colonial life was attractive to adventurous men of means, especially if they had family connections across the Atlantic, like Marr's Northumberland born relative, Captain Robert Fenwick, a seasoned colonial. Marr died in the early 1730s and left more than 1,500 acres of land and £500 to be divided between two sisters on Tyneside. His brother went out to Carolina to sell the property and Fenwick helped him.[83]

Part of Thomas Kitchin's map of North America, 1771. Many North Easterners landed in the southern states.

Thomas Monck, a soldier and politician, was amply rewarded by Charles II for helping him take the throne in 1660. As Lord Albemarle, Monck was given an eighth share in the newly captured colony of Carolina. Members of Monck's family crossed the Atlantic in the 1680s and settled in Berkeley County. During the next 20 years they acquired thousands of acres of land in Berkeley and adjoining counties and became leading 'planters' of sugar and indigo, the source of a much sought after blue dye. In 1740, another Thomas Monck married Joanne Broughton. Her grandfather and uncle, Sir Nathaniel and Robert Johnson, had been Governors of Carolina (the Johnsons were natives of Kibblesworth, a village just south of Gateshead) and another relative was a Newcastle Merchant Adventurer. This part of Carolina, near the capital Charleston, was where the Pinckneys (see page 104) from Bishop Auckland owned plantations, and Charles

97

Pinckney senior and Thomas Monck were partners in at least one deal. (In the late 18th century Sir Charles Monck inherited Belsay Castle in Northumberland.)[84]

The Colvilles were Newcastle merchants who were related to the Earls of Tankerville, of Chillingham Castle near Wooler in Northumberland. At least two Colvilles migrated to Virginia in the early 18th century. John Colville was a planter in St George's County by the 1720s and in the 1730s he tried trading in tobacco on the Potomac with his ship, *The Tankerville*. He became a large scale planter and land speculator and was estimated to own 20,000 acres of land and many slaves. He was a prominent figure in Virginia's civic life and a close friend of the Washingtons. (The Washington family were originally from County Durham. They emigrated to America in the 1670s.) Colville died in 1755, leaving his property to his brother Thomas, who had settled in Maryland, and Charles Bennet, Earl of Tankerville. Bennet also owned the Orchard Estate in Westmorland Parish, Jamaica, which was replete with slaves.

Courtesy of the Mount Vernon Ladies' Association

An idealised view of life in the colonies. Life of Washington – the Farmer, colour engraving by Claude Regnier after Junius Brutus Stearns, 1853.

12 Advantageous employments

North Eastern enterprise serviced the slave trade and the plantation economies. Economic migrants from the region owned slaves and traded in the products of slave labour.

In 1690 iron manufacturer Ambrose Crowley brought his technical and business skills from the South East to Wearside. A few years later he moved his business to the Derwent Valley, west of Newcastle, where he could conveniently buy fuel from the Durham coal barons and avoid the control of Newcastle's merchant guild.

The Crowley family bought homes in Whickham, including Whickham Manor, but their main properties were still in South East England and their major warehouses were on the Thames at Blackwall and Greenwich, so they maintained close connections with London's American and West Indian merchant community and the Atlantic. In 1711-16 Ambrose and his son were deeply involved in lobbying for the establishment of the South Sea Company, which bought the National Debt and acquired Spanish approval for a monopoly of slave trading operations south of the Equator for over 30 years.

Before his death in 1718 Crowley Ambrose had built what may have been the world's largest iron enterprise in and around the villages of Whickham, Swalwell and Winlaton. Over 2,000 artisans and labourers used cottage forges to produce a breathtaking variety of metal goods. Among those listed in an inventory compiled in 1739 are candlesticks, clout nails, combs, hoops, nippers, mincing knives, scythes, frying pans, iron crow, letter rings, trowels, plastering springs, latches, bolts, chisels, boilers, saws, staples, garden hoes, hinges, keys, clock plates, harrows, rings and bolts, rivets, sprockets, gunners forelocks, starting hammers, bottle hoops, thumb latches, scrapers, shovels, axes, adzes, coopers drawing knives, shovels, harpoons, saucepan holders, screws, goudges, knitting needles, shoe trimmers, tailors' sheers, forks, etc. Such items would be in great demand in the new territories across the Atlantic and in West Africa, where they were exchanged for Africans. Warehouse inventories also included South Sea

Locks made for Negroes Necks

	Doz:	odd
20×		2
1×	5	1
1c	4	10
1c	2	6
1/	1	6
c/	1	1
co/	1	

Flatt Stock Locks
Six in a Sheets

−o×		2
1/		1
1/		2
1/		1
1−		2
c×		1

Part of an inventory from Crowley's iron works, dating from 1739.

hatchets, South Sea axes in three sizes, four dozen Virginia narrow hoes, five dozen broad Virginia hoes, many dozens of narrow and broad Barbados hoes, four dozen broad Carolinas hoes, Jamaica ropes, tobacco knives, sugar shovels, locks for Negroes' necks, shackles, bilbos, port shackles, chains and branding irons CED/S, AE, cB,ER, RB, OB He, P and so on. The Crowleys owned 23 merchant ships, some of which must have worked the Atlantic run.[85]

Steel leg irons like these were probably produced by Crowley's works.

There were other entrepreneurs. In 1731 Robert Clarke, a ship owner and master mariner of North Shields, had *The Cleveland* specially fitted out for trading with Charleston, South Carolina. He was deeply involved in the London coal trade, very familiar with the merchant community and ideally placed to spot opportunities for international transactions.[86] William Cramlington, Merchant Adventurer, rope maker and one-time Mayor of Newcastle was the partner of Jonathan Blagdon, a carrier of coal and convicts to America. Cramlington had interests in the colonial world through his marriage to Ann Lake whose father was a landowner in North America.[87] The prominent Blackett family were early importers of rum from Jamaica. By 1740 there were over 100 sugar houses in Britain and by 1750 there was probably at least one in Newcastle.

On June 4, 1752: 'Was launched from Headlam's landing, upon the river Tyne, *The Experiment*, built by the gentlemen of Newcastle, subscribers to a West Indian trade.' We don't know who the 'gentlemen of Newcastle' were, but presumably they were Merchant Adventurers, since outsiders were apparently barred. The ship's name suggests that this form of trade was a new venture. On October 5 'this vessel commanded by Captain John Scaife, sailed on her first voyage to Jamaica.' On June 13, 1753, it 'arrived in the Tyne, after a passage of eight weeks, bringing a cargo of sugar, rum, pimento, coffee, cotton, mahogany and lignum vitae in return for the commodities and manufactures of Newcastle, which had been sent out.'[88]

In the *Newcastle Courant* of June 18, 1772, we read:

To any owner, fitter or builder,
WANTED by the end of August or first of September to charter for one year, a good North Country BARK that will carry from 500-600 hogsheads of Grenada sugar. If she is a compleat ship she will be settled in one of the first and most advantageous employments in England as the Charter has obtained a contract from the Island of Grenada for 600 hogsheads of sugar to be loaded on any ship she will bring to the Island every year in the month of May. Any principle [sic] person as above that will either build or charter an unexceptionable ship shall hear more by applying to Captain Resolve Smith at Lloyd's Coffee House, Lombard Street, London.

The short gap of two months between the advertisement and the required delivery date meant that only a 'compleat ship' could be ready in time. We can't presume that a ship was supplied from this advertisement but the Tyne was a major ship building river for ocean going craft.

In June 1776 *The Fly*, owned by a Mr Needham, and with Captain Wood as master, left the Tyne returning 12 months later. *The Fly*'s one-year absence suggests that it its first port of call was probably on the West African coast and that it sailed the Atlantic before returning to the Tyne.[89] This is the only evidence of a slave trader, being built on the Tyne or Wear, though other ships may have been adapted. Single-ownership was uncommon, since several people usually paid for one or more one-fortieth share of a vessel and a similar share of its profits. Direct slave trading from the North East would not make much business sense, because it would add around 1,000 miles to the Atlantic journeys and increase the hazards and expense. However, there was nothing to prevent Newcastle ships, and crews, moving into the trade from more appropriate ports like London.[90]

In 1760 Edward Cook, a farmer's son from Togston near Alnwick, went to farm and trade in Maryland with his cousins, William Ottley and William Batson. Cook was able to buy substantial tracts of land and in July 1761 he wrote to his brother: 'The Land here is Extreamly good in severall parts it might be purchased from 5s per Acre to £2 2s sterling it grows perdigious fine wheat.' He wrote regular optimistic letters to relatives, despite losing a ship:

> The 8th Inst. our partner Mr Batson arrived here from St Kitts in perfect health. He went super cargo in our snow [*a type of brig*] bound for Antigua but was Unfortunately disappointed by a small privateer of 4 Guns & 8 Swivells who took the Adventure within 12 leagues of Antigua, he was carryed into Martinica, he was used very well there he was upon Parole of Honour but not Satisfyed with it made his Escape to Slatia [*possibly the neutral Dutch island of Saint Eustatius*] & from thence he got to St Kitts where he see little Brown the corn factor in a very good way of Business. This unlucky affair has Turn'd our profitts a little over the left shoulder. Had we reached Antigua safe it would have turn'd out greatly to our Advantage.

Cook was clearly an economic migrant, but he had problems with finding labourers:

> Servants is hard to be got, convicts you pay for country business from £12 to £15 sterling for 7 Years servitude, Negroes from £40 to £60 sterling &

something more for Life. Farms to be taken for an Old Song W.O. took one the Other day about 900 Acres I suppose 300 cleared of wood for about £6:12 [sic] sterling per one year … Harvest people very Dear 2/- 8d sterling per day. All sorts of Mechanicks dear. Masons Brickmakers Bricklayers Carpenters Wheelwrights Shoemakers Barbers Gardeners Sadlers Watchmakers Butchers that has a good Stock pay cash Ship Carpenters would meet with good Encouragement … Building is going fast & cannot get Workmen. Blacksmith good Business as W. Hutson [*presumably an Alnwick man*] is a clever fellow he would make 5/- sterling per day.

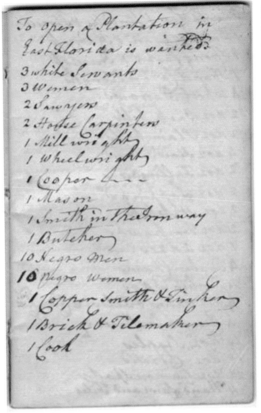

This list (written by Liverpool slave trader Joseph Manesty, see page 128) estimates the requirements for opening a plantation.

Northumberland Collections Service (2 DE 44-9)

He asked his brother:

> Can't you send us a Parcell of Good country men they will find good Encouragement and Live well, Masons bricklayer Wheelwrights & Joyners are much wanted. If any will Indent for three years I will give them 12 sterling per year and pay their passage from London. I must have one Good country man upon any Terms for our Overseers or Stewards here are writched creatures at Farming.

African slaves were clearly the best bet. Whilst they cost more to acquire than convicts or white indentured servants, you had them for life. Cook arrived when the demand for North American independence was rising. His mother and sister visited Maryland to review the situation, which suggests that he intended to stay, but either by coercion or choice he had returned to

Alnwick by 1776 and his Maryland property was sequestered. After the war ended his nephew, also Edward Cook, made an attempt to have the plantations returned. He pursued the matter through the courts but was largely unsuccessful. He probably lacked high status connections, though his advisor, Robert Ogle, was apparently a Northumberland-born settler.[91]

Early in the 18th century, possibly as a response to a dip in the Baltic trade caused by war between Russia and Sweden, the Newcastle merchant Ralph Carr attempted to supply the North American domestic market with coal. His letter books show that for more than 30 years his collier brigs crossed to New York, Boston and the Caribbean. Coal became an important source of domestic heating in the mainland North American colonies and a key fuel in sugar and rum production, because of its superiority over brushwood. Carr's ships returned with ballasts of pitch – a highly saleable product on a ship-building river. Very small amounts of coal had been discovered in Virginia in the 17th century, but modest commercial production did not start till the revolutionary crisis of the 1770s, and the Carrs' North American trade came to an abrupt end with the War of Independence.[92]

By the 1770s the North American roots of some former North East English people were generations deep. In 1691 Thomas Pinckney, a mariner from Bishop Auckland, County Durham, voyaged to Carolina and Jamaica. Two years later he returned to Carolina, married and began to grow tobacco. His wife died in 1695 and in 1697 he returned to Durham to marry Mary Cotesworth, whose surname became the middle name of their son and grandson. The Cotesworths were among Durham's most prominent merchants in the early 18th century, and were associated with the founding of the South Sea Company, so this advantageous marriage linked two wealthy families across the Atlantic. The North American Pinckneys built a great planter dynasty. Charles Pinckney, Thomas's son, married Elizabeth Lucas, a planter's daughter from Antigua, and she became a planter in her own right, farming indigo on a large scale. Their son, Charles Cotesworth Pinckney, went to England in the 1760s to be educated at Christchurch, Oxford. He developed a close friendship with Matthew White Ridley of

Newcastle.[93] After graduating in 1766, they set off together on a Grand Tour of Europe, and Charles spent time in Caen, training at the military academy. In the 1770s Pinckney become a General in Washington's Continental Army and a signatory from South Carolina of the Declaration of Independence.

Property of the Ridley family, Blagdon.

Charles Cotesworth Pinckney and Sir Matthew White Ridley (seated), around 1764, after graduation from Christchurch, Oxford, before their Grand Tour (detail). The artist is John Hamilton Mortimer.

Benjamin Stead inherited the Ryal Estate, near Matfen in Northumberland. He married Patience Wise Blackett, daughter of John Erasmus Blackett.[94] Stead was well connected to Blacketts, Roddams and Collingwoods in England and to Johnsons, Pinckneys and Izards in North America. His mother, Mary Johnson, was a daughter of a Governor of South Carolina. Charles Cotesworth Pinckney and Ralph Izard, another planter, married two of Stead's sisters. Pinckney and Izard would become the first senators from South Carolina to the US Congress.

Stead's father had left him extensive rice and sugar plantations in South Carolina and Georgia. During the War of Independence Stead was at college in England, but he and his new wife returned to what was now the United States in 1784.[95] The British had assumed that the Steads were rebels, killed the stock on his Georgia estates for food and freed the slaves. The Carolina estates had also been disrupted by the loss of slaves, but after the

British were defeated the authorities assumed that the Steads were loyal to the new regime and left them intact. The Georgia authorities meanwhile assumed the Steads had been loyal to the British, impounded his estates and sold them off. Stead complained to his father-in-law Blackett in Newcastle: 'The lands in Georgia are very valuable and well worth 15 gns per acre', yielding '4lbs of rice per acre.' He had '140 Negroes remaining' but 'many have not been apprehended.'[96]

Charles Pinckney took Stead's petition for restitution to the Georgia Assembly. The claim was only partly successful, though Pinckney told Stead that he believed 'there is no doubt I should be paid in some measure for the losses in this country from the British' and hoped for Blackett's help.[97] In 1787 Pinckney wrote warmly to Newcastle from Philadelphia, enquiring after the health of Matthew Ridley's wife and children, and sending a draft copy of the new Constitution of the United States for comments.[98] The loss of a brother in the war, not to mention the loss of the colonies, had apparently not dimmed the 20 year friendship.

Somewhat bruised by his reception in the USA, Stead returned to England in 1788 and bought a Hertfordshire estate. Presumably he lived off his plantation income, but his many complaints to Blackett over the years suggest that profits made from the sweat of English labourers did not match those from slaves, 33 of whom Pinckney sold off for him at Charleston in 1803.

Geography and traditional trading links limited the numbers who crossed the Atlantic from the North East, yet many did, and many more were connected with the New World through close relationships with the merchant communities of London and elsewhere. London was the political and business hub of the empire; Liverpool and Bristol had merchant houses entirely dedicated to the slave trade and the products of slavery, and Glasgow's wealth was created from tobacco imports from the colonies and exports of central Scotland's industrial products. Nevertheless North East England was a fully-paid-up member of the imperial mission. Newcastle may not be compared with the major centres of the British slavery business, but the region was involved to some extent and North Easterners, like all the other Britons, were implicated in the dirty trade of plantation production and the trade and consumption of its products.

By courtesy of Sir Hugh Blackett

John Erasmus Blackett, painted by David Martin. Blackett came to the North East after an apprenticeship with the leading Liverpool slave trader George Cunliffe (see page 127). For 60 years he was a prominent leader of business, political and social life on Tyneside. Newcastle's Blackett Street is named after him.

13 Wage slaves

The slave trade could not have existed without the participation of white, waged labour. From the 17th century, British ships heading for Africa were manned mainly by British sailors, mostly from the seafaring towns.

A preponderance of men from the south and west of England worked the Atlantic trade, and most goods left southern and western ports for Africa, the Caribbean and the American colonies, though Caribbean and North American seamen later became more common.

Tens of thousands of men were trained on the colliers, whalers and general merchant ships registered in North East ports and many sailed beyond the North Sea, the Channel and the Arctic. Some merchant shipping was interrupted by bitter winter conditions, so owners, sometimes captaining their own vessels, would sail the oceans looking for cargoes. They usually had pre-arranged destinations and purchasers on outward journeys, but returns could be speculative and related to changes in weather conditions, so Geordie seamen could find themselves almost anywhere in the world.

Robert Hutton was born at Stainton, North Yorkshire, in 1761. He was apprenticed to his uncle, a Sunderland coal trader, and soon after finishing his apprenticeship on a collier brig he rose up the merchant navy hierarchy, becoming captain of the *Nelly* in his mid-twenties. He developed a reputation for being determined to turn a profit from all voyages and never returning to port empty. After losing a collier in a Channel storm, he signed on as second mate on an Africa Company schooner, *The Spy*, commanded by a Captain Wood. Almost immediately the first mate left and Hutton took over that role. The surgeon died before they crossed the Atlantic and he did that job, too. Reportedly, he was particularly humane in his treatment of slaves and was praised for delivering the human cargo without loss of life. Evidently, the commander and crew members resented his treatment of slaves and tried to kill him. He overpowered two assailants and threw them overboard, and a third leapt to death. When he returned to London the commander accused him of murdering the men, but the Africa

This beautiful glass goblet, 25cm high, was made by the Newcastle glass-enameller Thomas Beilby in 1762. It marked the launch at Whitehaven, Cumbria, of the ship King George, which would become a slaver. The royal coat of arms is on one side and on the other is a sailing ship and 'Success to the African Trade of Whitehaven'. Ironically, Thomas Bewick would later be apprenticed to the Beilbys and would go on to engrave one of the most potent images of the abolition movement.

Company proprietors did not accept the charge. In fact, they offered him the position of Governor of their assets on the African coast at the enormous salary of £6,000 per annum, but apparently he declined in favour of learning the slave trade and commanding *The Spy*. In Africa he exchanged ivory, gold, trinkets and gold dust for hatchets, spades, buttons, dresses and suits, but in 1791 he died on board the slave ship he commanded on the way back from the Caribbean. His chest contained much less of value than would have been expected from a man in his position and so it is tempting to speculate that he might have been robbed and murdered.[99]

William Richardson was born in South Shields in July 1768.[100] Like the majority of the male population of the town his father was a mariner, though he commanded a ship from time to time. William was destined for a life at sea, but as one of seven children he was fortunate to be sent to school, six miles away at West Boldon. He enjoyed learning but the school did not teach navigation, so he acquired that knowledge in Shields before finishing his formal education in Newcastle. He had an exciting career. In 1780 he was apprenticed to a Newcastle coal trade captain and made regular journeys to London, Amsterdam and the Baltic, but in 1781, during the American War of Independence, he narrowly avoided being captured by privateers off the Norfolk coast. In 1785 he went to Memel in Prussia to pick up timber for Norfolk, then returned to Shields to load coal for Marseilles, where they took on cotton and sarsaparilla for London. In 1786 his ship called at Gibraltar, before crossing to the Barbary Coast. They stayed for a fortnight and enjoyed a meal in a Moroccan prince's camp. An English boy from a French brig introduced him to French cooking. He felt that 'a stewpan with live snails' was 'as eatable as periwinkles.' The ship was loaded with wheat, dates and beeswax. They crossed back to Gibraltar, where they hid two Jewish merchants who feared for their lives in Spain, delivered their cargo at Cadiz, loaded salt for Königsberg in the Baltic, went to Memel and loaded spars for Corunna in Spain, delivered an illicit shipment of 40,000 Spanish gold dollars to merchants in Exmouth, Devon – 'our young men found plenty of sweethearts among the Exmouth lasses' – and headed back to Shields.

In 1787 Richardson was on a boat taking coal to Cartagena. They loaded with salt, 'our captain intending to steer for Ireland or America, which ever the wind answered best', but it 'being inclined to the northward

Tyne and Wear Museums

'Slaver – all Black', painted by John Wilson Carmichael, early 19th century.

we steered for Philadelphia' and arrived in time for the Fourth of July celebrations. His account continues:

There is a kind of zig zag road about three or four miles long leading from the city to a place called the Schuykil, along which the procession was to go; and first went the different trades people in regular order, some on sledges working at their trades, with music playing and colours flying; next followed some heads and members of Congress in an open temple or rotunda drawn by horses, and occasionally handing out a glass of wine to one or another, with a tall man dressed in a coat of mail riding before them. But best sight was a little frigate, with all her sails set, drawn by thirteen horses, and so heavy that the people were obliged to keep throwing water on the axle trees to keep them from catching fire; many people were on the decks, some giving commands, some steering and some heaving the lead, but all this was matter of form.

That evening the road 'was covered with people reeling home, some drunk in the ditches and some lying stupid with bloody heads and noses.' They loaded flour and biscuit in barrels, crossed the Atlantic to Santander and saw bull baiting in the street. Then they returned to Shields, carrying ballast, and William ended his seven-year apprenticeship. His next trip took him to the River Thames and he 'took special notice of a fine ship fitting out there with a tier of gun ports and copper bottomed, a rare thing for a merchantman in those days'. He felt like a change and sought and achieved his captain's agreement to sign on to *The Spy*, unaware, he says, of its destination until the voyage was well under way. *The Spy* was a slave ship bound for the Guinea Coast.[101]

For North East seamen there were many opportunities for a change of scene, and even if they stuck to the normal coastal routes they were in London between four and six times a year. The Thames riverside was a global microcosm where young men would meet sailors from across the world, and the dirty, dangerous and mundane run from Tyne to Thames might prompt fantasies about the New World, the tropics and bounty. Conditions were harsh on merchant ships. Sailors had to climb about in the rigging in high seas, eat poor food, suffer ritual bullying, accept low wages and cope with the fear of piracy and an early, watery grave. Some men volunteered for, or were pressed into, the Navy, but it tended to decommission ships at the end of wars. That left sailors jobless and on the look out for new opportunities, but not necessarily anywhere near their home port, since some of the most important Navy bases were at Chatham, Sheerness, Portsmouth and Plymouth. Finding a new berth meant taking what was available. But slave ships were especially alienating. Sailors were required to be not only gaolers but also to reshape the captives' identities in preparation for their new existence on the far side of the Atlantic. Sailors would apply the chains when slaves arrived on board, shave their bodily hair, sluice down their bodies, force feed them when necessary, make them sing and dance with the cat-o-nine tails, apply the lash for disciplinary infractions and oil and polish them for the market. Sailors might also be required to weed out the infirm and toss them overboard. Drowning was an insurable death, unlike disease, so the slave traders' profits wouldn't suffer. One historian describes Africans going through an experience of social death as they were systematically broken from the customs and practices of their homes and families. Apparently, few seamen had the stomach for multiple voyages.[102]

Richardson made few disapproving remarks about the slave trade, but its appalling nature was obvious. When preparing the ship for receiving slaves, the crew:

> clear the decks of all lumber, and a barricade is built across the main deck near the mainmast about ten feet high, with wall pieces fixed upon the top to fire among the slaves if necessary and a small door to let one man through at a time ... The 'tween decks were entirely cleared fore and aft, and a platform fixed round against the ships sides and hung on cranks, height about half way between the two decks: this is for the slaves to sleep upon that had not room on the lower deck ...

He describes a raiding party at New Calabar. War canoes with three pounders strapped in the bows proceeded up river, concealing themselves in woods near a village, and at nightfall:

Wooden manacles, probably for the feet, thought to have been made in Angola in the 1700s.

> they rushed on the poor inhabitants ... made them all prisoners (except old men and old women, as they were not saleable.) They continued their depredations night after night for near a fortnight, and then they returned with their canoes full of slaves ... shouting and rejoicing as if they had gained a great victory.

Captured West Africans marching to the coast.

Richardson evidently remained on the ship.

> During the first two months they were brought to us pretty regularly, and I suppose we must have got two hundred of both sexes, but after that they came slowly. Poor creatures! It was pitiful to see the distress they were in on coming aboard, for some of them think that we live on the ocean and wanted them for food. Some of the females fainted, and one of them went out of her mind; we did all we could to comfort them, and by degrees they got more composed.

It took six months running down the Guinea coast for the ship to be filled to its capacity of 450 slaves, but casualties among slaves and sailors were high.

When the ship was ready they 'steered to the southwards for what is called the middle passage to the West Indies' and 'it was pitiful to see the poor slaves with their eyes full of tears, looking to the land as long as a bit of it was to be seen; the females wept bitterly.' He is silent on conditions below deck.

Anti-Slavery International

African men are forced below deck on a slave ship.

In the mornings, when the decks are all washed and dried, the slaves were all ordered up on the upper deck; the men were all arranged in line along both sides of the main deck; they were shackled together two each by the legs and then a long deck chain on each side was rove through a ring at each shackle and

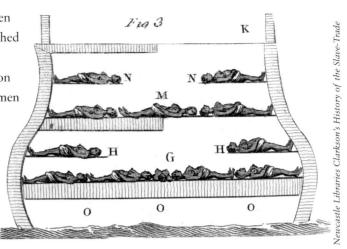

This cutaway image of the women's deck from the Brooks slave ship, from Clarkson's History of the Slave-Trade, indicates the overcrowding below deck.

Newcastle Libraries Clarkson's History of the Slave-Trade

secured at both ends, so that the poor fellows could only sit or stand; in the evening the deck chains were unrove and they were sent below, but still having their shackles on; the females are never shackled … for they assist to get up wood and water and to peel the yams; when all were got below in the evenings the gratings were put over and well secured and the watch set.

Unsurprisingly, slaves tried to escape, usually with fatal consequences, as when two 'prime females' managed to slip overboard but 'the poor creatures' were torn to pieces by sharks within a few yards of the ship 'and not a fragment of them [was] to be seen except the water tinged with their blood'. Richardson wrote disapprovingly of the captain's savagery towards a female slave who had concealed a knife on her person:

He had her seized up by both hands to the main rigging, then stripping off his upper garment he began to flog the poor creature over her naked back with a cat-of-nine-tails until he was tired; he then stopped to rest a while, and began again, and I doubt if he would have left off until he nearly killed the poor creature, had it not been for the cries and lamentations of the other female slaves, who stood near, the poor creature having fainted.

The Atlantic journey ended at Montego Bay, Jamaica. Richardson took a company of slaves into town, unshackled, partly to let them get their land legs, but 'more with the intent of letting the planters see what fine slaves we had got'. At the slave market, they were:

> all put into a dark room and the planters have each as many tallies as they want slaves in number. They are then admitted into the dark room, where they cannot see to pick and choose, and each ties his tallies to the neck of the slaves that he gets among; they are them brought out … they are sold at the rate of £44 each …

The ship was given a good cleaning, carefully loaded with sugar, rum and mahogany, and then they headed for Britain, arriving some ten months after they left.

The tone of Richardson's account is sympathetic to the Africans and, unlike other whites, he seemed not to question their humanity. We cannot know how typical this attitude was among ordinary seamen, because so few accounts have survived. Captains and owners had a vested interest in dousing any fellow-feeling between sailors and slaves, as sailors were certainly exploited and oppressed. 'The owners though floating in wealth were very hard on poor sailors at this time, not shipping them till the last minute and then giving them low wages.' Most masters considered them to be very low life specimens who could be bullied with impunity. Mutinies were not uncommon on general merchant ships, and often the first step on the road to piracy, but despite the savagery meted out by the captains they were extremely rare on slave ships. The 'property' in the holds was rightly seen as a dynamic source of danger to all white men on board, but creating instability was a terrible gamble, and sailors' violent impulses were much more likely to be taken out on the slaves than on captain and officers. The fundamental insecurity created by holding masses of angry and querulous human beings in restricted space for months on end was probably a potent source of racist sentiment amongst the crew.

The polarities of white versus black and free versus slave probably induced sailors to come to the aid of slave ship captains facing slave insurrections. Richardson witnessed a revolt of slaves on a French slaver moored off Bonny and expressed some admiration and even sympathy for the Africans, but he had no doubt that the uprising had to be put down and punishment meted out as a deterrent. Like most sailors who had been on a slaver once, he did not want to make a second trip, but in a moment of

An insurrection on board a slave ship, 1787, an illustration in William Fox's 'Brief History of the Wesleyan Missions', 1851. The crew are firing upon the rebel Africans.

penury he signed up for another voyage of 'the barbarous trade', only to see the vessel develop serious problems at Ostend, so the journey was not continued.

Richardson had an eventful period sailing to the East Indies, suffering a ship wreck and two impressments, but he did learn how to make his own clothes. In 1793, at the start of the war with France, he sailed to Britain on a Navy frigate, *Minerva*, and later served in the Caribbean, where he had several encounters with the French, including a successful attempt to capture and impound a warship. In 1800 he was posted to a prison ship moored off Martinique, an island that had been captured from the French, and participated in suppressing a rebellion of black French prisoners who had been agitated by Napoleon's reversal of the revolutionaries' decision to emancipate French-owned slaves. He had met men of all nationalities in London and other European ports, visited British slave trader ports, routinely sailed beyond the North Sea and Baltic, occasionally crossed the Atlantic and was subject to low wages, periods of unemployment and impressments. His experience was probably typical of many.[103]

Samuel Robinson, of Wigton near Carlisle, was 14 when he made his first voyage to Africa. Shortage of crew was always a problem for slave ships, and that made berths available for the desperate and the naïve. Samuel thought it would be an adventure, but before they reached Guinea the captain ordered him to give another youth twelve strokes with the cat for no apparent reason, or he would get 24 himself. He flogged the boy until blood ran from the stripes on his back and then the captain ordered the flogged boy to give Samuel 12 strokes. He was reeling from the pain when a sympathetic seaman whispered that the captain wanted to see them fight or he would order further flogging. Terrified, Samuel hit his mate in the face and wrestled him to the deck, and eventually the other boy submitted. He was tied to the mast and flogged again. The only medicine was a tot of rum. (It is hard to see this brutal sadism as anything other than a cynical initiation into what would be expected of young white sailors when confronted by black prisoners.) Robinson wrote of the seamen's philosophy of life, including his tendency to spend his wages only hours after hitting land. Any prospect of making a way home could be quickly drowned in the dockside bars and this made a seaman vulnerable to the Navy press gang or being shanghaied by 'crimps' onto a slave ship.[104]

Wage slaves were not only employed at sea. Some people went as labourers to the plantations. The Hendersons of Felton near Morpeth were not well off when they arrived in Jamaica in 1837. William Henderson was asked 'to overlook the estate and work in the Garden occasionally and to brew Malt drink'. He was promised 'wages £40 per year' and 'victualling for all the family'. 'Catharine can if she thinks proper be employed in the laundry.' They would have 'a comfortable house and firing, liberty to keep pigs and poultry, a large garden to raise vegetables for the use of pigs, all expenses paid on our passage out' and 'medical attendance free of expense. Should the country not agree with us after one years trial or any dislike to live longer there our passage paid home to England.' He later reported: 'It is a good country for an industers [sic] man for anything that you put in the ground it will grow.'[105] Unusually, this manual worker's family was literate and wrote letters that give us a vivid picture of the lives of white people low down in the social hierarchy.[106]

14 Newcastle's West Indiaman

West India merchants were common in Bristol, Liverpool and London but in the North East only one seems to merit the description. He was hardly a minor figure though, with his extensive interests in Jamaica and the North East and Yorkshire.

John Graham was born in 1736 near Beverley in Yorkshire.[107] His mother, formerly Dorothy Clarke, came from a Sutton family prominent enough to register a coat of arms. There was a cluster of property-owning Clarkes in the Sutton-Beverley area and the family had connections with the Hull merchant community through Thomas Mowld (possibly John's great uncle) and John Graves. In 1757, when Britain was engaged in the Seven Years War, an Act of Parliament compelled all able-bodied men aged between 18 and 50 to be part of a ballot for the Militia, with a proportion of them required to enlist for three years.

In 1760 Graham was selected by ballot and became a junior officer in the East Yorkshire Grenadier Militia, which meant that his annual income must have been at least £50. He served in Colonel Grimston's Company and appears to have developed a friendship with the Grimston family, who lived at Anlaby Hall near Hull. The Militia Act was unpopular, especially in farming communities where strong young men were at a premium, and it was possible for young men to be sent to fight abroad, so it provoked considerable resistance. There were, as yet, no barracks in Newcastle and officers were commonly billeted with local families. Graham met and married Elisabeth Rutter, who owned the town's main brewery. Her late husband, Charles Rutter, had been a prosperous Newcastle brewer, baker and member of the merchant guild.

Kenton Lodge around 1795.

It is interesting that a young man in his twenties, and a newcomer to the area, could insert himself so effectively into the business and social community of Newcastle. Graham's career throws light on the important transition from merchant to industrial capitalism. Within a few years he apparently enjoyed the trust of old merchant families, including the Ridleys, Surtees, Hedleys, Blacketts, Rankins and Forsters. In the 1760s owning a large brewery could ensure a comfortable lifestyle, but Graham needed capital to purchase a glassworks and build new premises on Pilgrim Street, near the brewery. He was considered to be a reliable shareholder in the Burdon & Surtees Bank as early as 1771. Elisabeth died that year and Graham inherited her property. In 1774 he subscribed to the new Newcastle Infirmary and in 1776 he was an original subscriber to the new Assembly Rooms and the person delegated to receive other subscriptions. He had a counting house in Pilgrim Street and owned several ships, including the *Arabella*, *Rebecca*, *David Lyon* and *Kingston* (possibly named after the Jamaican town).

Arabella Altham was the daughter of Roger and Mary (Isaacson)

Altham of Islington in London, and the younger sister of Mary who married the Newcastle banker, Aubone Surtees the younger. (Surtees' sister, Bessie, was married to John Scott, who as Lord Eldon, was to become Lord Chancellor of England.) In 1782 Graham married Arabella, even though she was some 25 years younger than he, and this marriage, like the first, was financially advantageous. As part of his daughter's marriage settlement, Roger Altham gave £1,500 in South Sea consoles, which were almost always bound up with the Caribbean and the slave trade. That year Graham acquired the name and arms of 'Clarke' by the terms of Thomas Mowld's will and became John Graham Clarke. He also benefited from the will of a Mrs Mary Graves, a widow of Hull, who had been Thomas Mowld's housekeeper.

Over the next 10 years Roger Altham made equal settlements on his five daughters. Apart from South Sea consoles, a very important feature was a share of the large Fenton and Nesbitt Estate in North Northumberland. That district was noted for progressive farming practice, and the estate of the leading innovator, William Culley, adjoined Fenton. Rapid enclosure and farming rents provided a growing part of landed incomes, and when Roger Altham died a few years later he left John Graham Clarke another £1,000 in South Sea consoles and a share – at least – of the Fenton estate.

Many Cumbrians had supported the 1745 Jacobite rebellion and 20-year-old Jacob Graham – John Graham's uncle – appears to have left Brampton for Jamaica in 1746.[108] He lived in St James's parish and became a slave trader, overseer, book-keeper, manager and ultimately a plantation owner. He settled near the estates of the Barretts, one of the most prominent planter families, with plantations in St James, Trelawney and St Ann's parishes on the island's north side. In 1792 the six children of the late George Goodin Barrett and Elissa Peters, a slave woman, were sent to live with Jacob Graham's nephew, John Graham Clarke in Newcastle. By the terms of Barrett's will their mother received an annuity, a house and three black girls – presumably slaves – as servants. The six children were to be freed from slavery and 'decently clothed maintained and educated in a moral manner'. They should 'not fix their abode in Jamaica but do settle and reside in such countries where those distinctions respecting colour are not maintained.' They were to receive annuities on becoming 21 and Thomas, the eldest, was also to be a trustee of the Jamaican estates.

We know that Graham Clarke visited Jamaica in the early 1790s, and planter families evidently found him a helpful friend. In 1793 a Newcastle trade directory lists him as a 'West India Merchant'. On February 8, 1794 an advertisement in the *Newcastle Chronicle* announced:

Another long-standing planter family in northern Jamaica was the Scarletts. When 15-year-old James Scarlett went to England in 1785 to begin his education, he headed to the Graham Clarke household in Newcastle and became a regular guest during vacations. In the mid-1790s Scarlett acted as ward for the young Edward Moulton Barrett, who was newly arrived from Jamaica, and the Graham Clarkes played host to him at their new home, Kenton Lodge, where Scarlett met Mary, their eldest daughter.

In October 1797 'The *Rebecca*, owner Mr John Graham Clarke is recorded as arriving in the Tyne with a cargo of Jamaica rum sold for £363.14.5 on the estate of Jarvis Gallimore on the account of James Scarlett, Josh Lubbren [sic] and Christopher Blackett'. Gallimore was Scarlett's mother's maiden name and Christopher Blackett was the major Newcastle importer of rum.

In 1806 Mary Graham Clarke and Edward Moulton Barrett married at Gosforth Parish Church. Although there is evidence of affection in the union it also brought together two families who had had a business arrangement for at least two decades. The Barretts were major land owners in Jamaica but apparently had no home in England until Edward Moulton Barrett got Coxhoe Hall for himself and his new wife. Theirs was a conventional marriage settlement, and Coxhoe may have been part of it, but the balance of advantage seems to have gone to Graham Clarke, who now

John Graham Clarke and his wife Arabella, after whom he named one of his ships.
Reproduced from 'The Family of the Barrett' by Jeanette Marks, 1938.

had improved access to Barrett's Jamaican holdings and their products. The
nature of the relationship is implied in Barrett's complaint in a letter of his
father-in-law's readiness to pay him what he was owed for imported sugar,
while wishing the complaint to remain secret. Their daughter, Elizabeth
Barrett – the future poet Elizabeth Barrett-Browning – was born in 1807.

Leonard Parkinson had spent a lifetime as a planter in Jamaica, where
he had been the Barrett family's business partner and had procured annual
commissions, possibly with the connivance of John Graham Clarke. On
returning to England, Parkinson bought the Frocester Estate in
Gloucestershire and Kinnersley Castle, Herefordshire.

Graham Clarke was very active in securing satisfactory business matches
for his own children, and in 1811 John Altham Graham Clarke, his heir,
married Mary Elizabeth Parkinson, Leonard's daughter. He received 500
acres of land at Frocester and the couple lived there. John Altham embarked
on the life of a country gentleman, spending freely, which apparently
irritated his father.

John Graham Clarke was an enthusiastic granter of mortgages. His
brother in law, Aubone Surtees, as well as Leonard Parkinson, Jacob
Graham, possibly Joseph Graham, a Jamaican cousin, Lord Chancellor

Eldon, several Barretts and sundry Jamaican planters appear to have been in his debt. He rented out land in Jamaica to the Morpeth gentleman, William Carr Walker, which Walker may have worked himself.

Jacob Graham died in 1816 and bequeathed his large Jamaican plantations, Lapland and Bamboo, to John Graham Clarke, and his houses and land to the six mulatto Barrett children who lived with him.

In 1816 Graham Clarke was elected as the first President of Newcastle Chamber of Commerce, but late that year he had the second of two strokes and became somewhat incapacitated. Late in 1817 he wrote a codicil to his will which drastically reduced his eldest son John Altham Graham Clarke's inheritance. A clerk recalled him saying that 'he's got enough already'.[109] John Graham Clarke died in 1818 and bequeathed between £7,000 and £10,000 to each of his five daughters. He owned three substantial properties on Pilgrim Street, Newcastle; mansions at Fenham Hall and Kenton Lodge; 200 acres in the East Riding of Yorkshire; and the Frocester Estate near Gloucester. He had also been a trustee of the Fenton and Nesbitt Estate at Wooler, Northumberland. He owned a brewery, flax mills and sugar houses on both sides of the Tyne, Coxlodge colliery and the Northumberland Glass Company at Lemington and Ouseburn. He had dabbled in rum imports, possessed at least four ships and had a share in the Burdon & Surtees Bank. A lawyer noted: 'Mr Graham Clarke is a very rich man. He has assets of £200,000 or thereabouts,' equivalent to perhaps £20 million today. His wider family had connections with at least 15 properties in Jamaica and the most likely explanation for this great wealth is that some of the Caribbean interests registered in his will were of very long standing, possibly even preceding his arrival in Newcastle in 1761.

A Jamaican rebel slave named Leonard Parkinson (possibly named after Jamaica planter Leonard Parkinson). He was known as 'Captain of the Maroons' and was hanged in 1795 following the second Maroon War.

University of Virginia Library, http://hitchcock.itc.virginia.edu/slavery/index.php

15 Estates at home and abroad

In common with other members of the British aristocracy and gentry, many wealthy North Easterners and their families had interests in the American and West Indian colonies. Some owned plantations, some owned ships trading between the colonies and Britain and were concerned with importing and distributing the products of slave labour. Often we can identify the connection by the family name, sometimes still familiar in the region today. It is much more difficult, usually impossible, to trace details of shareholding or to quantify how much their fortunes amounted to. The slavery compensation records offer a glimpse of the sums involved but other information is scarce and arrived at by chance.

Wallington Hall occupies one of the most beautiful sites in North East England. The elegant house can be seen on a hill a mile off the Newcastle to Otterburn road. The drive runs over an elegant 18th century bridge and alongside an unfenced lawn. Visitors can ramble for hours in the

Sally Mitchison

Wallington Hall, Northumberland.

Thought to be a portrait by Arthur Devis of Sir John Trevelyan, his wife Louisa Simond and family at Nettlecombe.

woods, linger by the pond and walk through the lovely walled garden and ancient hot houses with sub-tropical plants. In the house there are rooms that feel vaguely lived in, as if the owners had just gone off on a long vacation. The later generations of the Trevelyan family who lived there were liberal and radical. In 1934 Sir Charles Trevelyan, who had been a minister in Labour Governments, was the first landed gentleman to give his estate and its contents to the nation.

From the late 17th century the Blackett family at Wallington Hall was split geographically into three branches: Wallington and Newcastle; Matfen and Allendale; and Newby Hall, Yorkshire. The branches were connected by marriages and financial links, but lines died out and surnames changed. Surviving account books detail income from the coal trade, agricultural rents and the mining and sale of lead, but they also include profits from Bordeaux wine and Jamaican rum.[110]

The Newby Hall Blacketts were linked to one of England's major planter and slave trader families, the Lascelles of Barbados and Harewood near Leeds. It may have been this connection that enabled John Erasmus Blackett of Newby Hall to get an apprenticeship in Sir George Cunliffe's African Trade merchant house in Liverpool. After his apprenticeship, aged 25, John Erasmus (portrait on page 1107) moved to Newcastle and became a Merchant Adventurer and business manager for his Wallington Hall cousins. He was noted for speculative ventures. His cousin, Christopher Blackett, was a Newcastle merchant, a coal owner and exporter, and the region's major importer of Jamaican rum.[111]

The Blacketts were linked by marriage to the Delavals of Seaton Delaval. Sir Edward Blackett of Newby Hall married Diana, the widow of Sir Ralph Delaval in 1676. The Delaval family needed money and Sir John owed Sir Edward Blackett £14,000 (more than £1,000,000 at today's values). Sir John was succeeded by another Delaval who knew how to spend, but not how to accumulate, and the ensuing chronic financial crisis[112] may explain the family's long-established interest in land in North Carolina, where, in 1734 they appear to have fallen foul of the Governor, a former Durham man, Gabriel Johnson.

Newcastle Libraries

The crumbling magnificence of Seaton Delaval Hall around 1910.

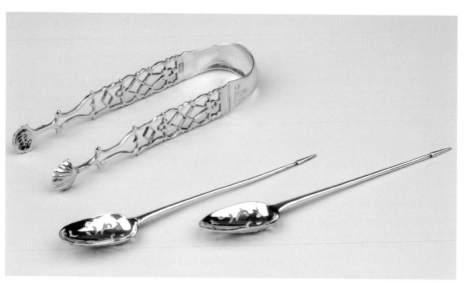

Tyne and Wear Museums

These silver sugar tongs, dating to around 1765, and the accompanying silver mote spoons (to skim off tea leaves) represent some of the luxury items associated with tea and sugar.

In the 1760s, at the end of the Seven Years War, Spain ceded Florida to the English Crown. This encouraged emigration and settlement. In 1766 Sir John Hussey Delaval sought advice from a Liverpool Slave trader, Joseph Manesty, on setting up and managing a plantation. Manesty replied with a list of requirements (pictured on page 103) including 'ten Negro men' and 'ten Negro women.' No detailed records have been found, but the Delavals seem to have taken the advice and hung on to the property until Florida reverted to Spain after the War of Independence in 1783.[113]

In 1757, John, the fourth Trevelyan baronet, married Luisa (Louise) Marianne Simond, the daughter of J.-P. Simond, a London merchant and Grenada sugar plantation owner. She brought her fortune into the Trevelyan family. The plantations were so distant from the English shires that moral dilemmas were seldom recorded and there is silence in the records about the fate of slaves. The West Indies connection was compounded by the marriage of Sir John's sister, Charlotte, to Tobias Frere, a Barbados planter who had a family connection with the Ridleys of Blagdon.[114] In 1768 Frere complained to his brother-in-law of 'money matters' and 'the failure of my

Above: a punchbowl made in Newcastle 1800-1833. Many punch ingredients, including rum, were Caribbean in origin. The ladle is silver and whalebone (about 1780).

Right: A sugar basket made by Francis Solloman, Newcastle upon Tyne, 1780.

Crop abroad which calamity has been universal throughout the Islands, makes it very inconvenient to raise so much cash.' His visit to Barbados the following year was cut short by his wife's illness.[115]

Sir John Trevelyan later ordered major renovations on the family's other great estate at Nettlecombe in Somerset.

> In 1776 he purchased a marble chimney piece inlaid with Sicilian jasper and in 1787 he employed Samuel Heal to make mahogany doors, fluted Ionic columns architraves and columns. He also employed John Vietch to landscape the park and grounds and lay out the great kitchen garden. He also built the stable block …
>
> He had served as Sheriff of Somerset, an expensive business as shown by surviving bills for twenty two sets of livery for the bailiffs, coachmen, and javelin men, a suit of clothes for the captain of the horse and a suit, gown and cassock for the chaplain.'[116]

Family correspondence indicates that Sir John, the 4th baronet, preferred Nettlecombe to Wallington (which he inherited in 1777 from his uncle Sir Walter Blackett). His attention to it supports this view. Yet it did not deter him from seeking to represent Newcastle in Parliament. In 1777 he importuned the Carpenters Guild for their support to succeed his uncle. Their minute book records his request. 'Permit me to

Tyne and Wear Museums

This gentleman's mahogany dressing table and washstand may have been custom-built for a North East family around 1800. This type of 'Spanish' mahogany was imported from Jamaica, Cuba and San Domingo from the 1700s. The cultivation and felling of the wood was dependant upon slave labour.

console upon the death of the late and highly honoured representative … (may I entertain) … a modest wish that I might be thought worthy to supply the vacancy in Parliament.'[117] He was elected in the General Election of that year, the only Newcastle Member of Parliament known to have had a West India interest.

In the large entrance hall of Wallington Hall are massive cabinets along two walls, which contain a remarkable collection of ceramics. Most of it was brought to Wallington in 1791 as part of the dowry of Maria Wilson, the London banker and East India trader's daughter. She married Sir John Trevelyan the 5th baronet. Her mother had built the collection over a period of 50 years and it represents the very best that China had produced from the 17th century, plus extremely choice pieces of Dutch, German, French and early English pottery. The furnishings, carpets, silver-ware, portrait paintings and the rest of the house's artefacts are of the same extremely high quality.

Just after Maria arrived at Wallington there was a great slave rebellion on Grenada. The Governor, Ninian Home of Paxton House near Berwick, was killed, and 60 plantations were wrecked. It took several months for the army and militia to regain control, but only after killing hundreds of slaves, either in conflict or by execution, and by selling others to planters on other islands. No records survive describing the family's reaction.

If the Trevelyan family had been able to read *The Grenada Free Press* 40 years later in 1833, they might have felt a little anxious. 'As far as our information reaches, the field people on many estates turned out lazily on Friday last (August 1st) and were vociferous in their expression of discontent' at being called 'free', since they 'must work still'. At one estate, 'they refused to work and were very insolent to and abusive to white people when they endeavoured to prevail upon them to go to the field.'[118]

Research for the Remembering Slavery Project (2007-8) highlighted a little-known part of Trevelyan history: their long term Caribbean connection. By 1820 they were partners in seven Grenada plantations which yielded great wealth. Under the great Emancipation Act of 1834 slave owners were required to register claims for compensation with an office at the Treasury in London. The claims from Grenada include seven made in the name of Trevelyans and their partners. They claimed for 1,240 slaves and £35,000, which at 2008 values would be around £3,000,000.

Uncontested Trevelyan claims (Grenada)

Claim 435:

John Alexander Hankey [*the Hankeys were business partners*]; Sir William Edward Rouse Boughton, bart; Sir Robert Heron, bart; Harriet Trevelyan, widow [*mother of Charles Edward*]; John Thomas Trevelyan; George Trevelyan; J. Trevelyan; W. Trevelyan; Thompson Hankey; The Rt hon Sir William Alexander, knight
joint claim for 240 slaves, award: £6,543.5.11

Claim 445:

John Alexander Hankey; Sir William Edward Rouse Boughton, bart; Sir Robert Heron, bart; Harriet Trevelyan, widow; John Thomas Trevelyan; George Trevelyan; John Trevelyan [*probably 5th baronet*]; Walter Trevelyan [*son of 5th baronet*]; Thomson [sic] Hankey; The Rt hon Sir William Alexander, knight
joint claim for 168 slaves, award: £4,499.16.1

Pepper pots made in England 1790-1810. Although most pepper came from the east, it was also grown in the Americas

Claim: 608

Charlotte Lushington; Augusta Lushington
joint claim for 124 slaves, award: £3,201.2.4

Claim: 760

John Alexander Hankey; Sir William Edward Rouse Boughton, bart; Sir Robert Heron, bart [*proprietor of Chipchase Castle, Northumberland*]; Harriet Trevelyan, widow; John Thomas Trevelyan; George Trevelyan; John Trevelyan; Walter Trevelyan; Thompson Hankey; The Rt hon Sir William Alexander, knight
joint claim for 14 slaves, award: £356.1.3

Claim: 771

John Alexander Hankey; Sir William Edward Rouse; Boughton, bart; Sir Robert Heron, bart; Harriet

This sugar bowl was made by a Newcastle silversmith in the mid-1700s. Sugar formed an important part of the triangular trade, and was a most profitable export from the Caribbean.

Trevelyan, widow; John Thomas Trevelyan;
George Trevelyan; John Trevelyan; Walter
Trevelyan; Thomson Hankey; The Rt hon Sir
William Alexander, knight
joint claim for 143 slaves, award: £4,195.6.10

Claim 857
John Alexander Hankey; Sir William Edward
Rouse Boughton, bart; Sir Robert Heron,
bart; Harriet Trevelyan, widow; John Thomas
Trevelyan; George Trevelyan; John Trevelyan;
Walter Trevelyan; Thomson Hankey; The Rt
hon Sir William Alexander, knight
joint claim for 208 slaves, award: £5,552.10.4

Claim 860
John Alexander Hankey; Sir William Edward;
Rouse Boughton, bart; Sir Robert Heron,
bart; Harriet Trevelyan, widow; John Thomas
Trevelyan; George Trevelyan; John Trevelyan;
Walter Trevelyan; Thomson Hankey; The Rt
hon Sir William Alexander, knight
joint claim for 231 slaves, award: £5,844.18.8

All images on these pages Tyne and Wear Museums

*This elaborate knife box was
made in England around 1780. It
is made of mahogany, which
became the most popular wood
for furniture making in the
1700s.*

*A snuff-box made out of a silver
mounted tortoise-shell formed
as a tortoise on four wheels. It
was presented to the vestry of
the parish of All Saints,
Newcastle, in 1828. It was made
in York about 1790. Tobacco
was another commodity of the
Caribbean and the Americas.*

Correspondence between Charles Edward Trevelyan and his mother and his business partner, Thompson Hankey, in the early 1840s suggests that the family's annual income had been at least equal to the compensation claim. They and their partners had been absentee owners and they lived very well from the proceeds of slavery.[119] As late as 1852 correspondence was taking place between Charles Edward and MacLeod of MacLeod, a friend and business partner, regarding one estate, the Tempe. He recommends the introduction of piece work, 'There can be no doubt as to the superior advantage of that mode of getting work done over Daywork.' He concludes that he has confidence that the Manager, Mr Haywood, 'will introduce it as far as he can without endangering the interests of the Proprietors or interfering too much with the prejudices of the Negroes.'[120] The latest evidence of continued Grenadian interest is in a letter from 1860 referring to a half yearly payment of an annuity to Miss H.C. Trevelyan from 'the West Indian Estate.'[121] There is no indication if, or when, these interests came to an end.

Only ten miles from Wallington is Brinkburn Priory, for centuries one of several Fenwick family homes. One, apparently Catholic, branch of the family had emigrated to Maryland before the English Civil War to become tobacco planters and merchants. Another planted rice near Charleston, South Carolina, building a grand plantation house which survives today on St Mary's Island. John Fenwick, a soldier in Cromwell's army, took refuge in New Jersey in the 1660s founding a Quaker colony. Another John Fenwick was a Baptist, an attorney and a leading member of the Newcastle anti-slavery movement in the 1830s. In the early 19th century, when the line of Fenwicks at Brinkburn was beginning to die out, the estate was sold to a London merchant, then to a Newcastle gentleman, and in 1825 to Ward Cadogan.

The Cadogans had been one the most powerful families in Stuart England and were very active in building the early empire. Some headed for Barbados. In 1815 Ward Cadogan's assets included the large Pickerings Plantation with its hundreds of slaves. He brought one slave, called Barrington, to England. In 1825 he granted Barrington his freedom.

Opposite, part of the manumission document which granted freedom to Barrington, should he return to the Caribbean.

Northumberland Collections Service ZFE 8

To all to whom these Presents shall come

late of the Island of Barbados but at present residing in the Town of London in the County of Devon &c—

Ward Cadogan of the City of Bath in that part of the United Kingdom of Great Britain and Ireland called England sends greeting— Whereas the said Ward Cadogan is seized to him and his Heirs in the Fee simple of the Slave hereafter described whom he is desirous of manumitting Now knowye. and these presents Witness that the said Ward Cadogan for and in consideration of the many true and faithful Services which he has experienced of and from a certain Negro Man Slave named Barrington since he became his Slave and also in consideration of the sum of ten shillings of lawful Money of the United Kingdom of Great Britain and Ireland of English value and currency to the said Ward Cadogan in hand paid by or on the behalf of the said Negro Man Slave named Barrington at or before the sealing and delivery of these Presents the Receipt whereof the said Ward Cadogan doth hereby expressly acknowledge and for divers other good and valuable causes and considerations thereunto moving He the said Ward Cadogan hath manumitted enfranchised released exonerated and for ever set free the

Newcastle Libraries (local coloured print)

Brinkburn in around 1830.

Cadogan's son-in-law and grandson carried out a large restoration project on the medieval Priory with the guidance of the celebrated Newcastle architect, John Dobson. It is likely that Barbados sugar money provided the funds. Under the 1834 Emancipation Act, the Cadogan family and their partners claimed compensation for the loss of 1,000 slaves and £25,000 – worth perhaps £2,500,000 today – and profits from sugar were figuring in family accounts in the 1850s.[122] Indeed the family owned Pickerings into the middle of the 20th century and their lives there are recorded in four family photograph albums.[123]

As we have noted earlier, Charles Bennet, Earl of Tankerville, owned the Orchard Estate in Westmorland Parish, Jamaica and acquired a share in his deceased brother's Virginia, and possibly Maryland, plantations. Some of these resources must have been used on the extensive Chillingham Estates in north Northumberland.

Opposite, part of an inventory of slaves on the Pickerings Plantation, Barbados for New Year's Day, 1817. The inventory continues on the following pages. The list of Cadogan property provides a very vivid picture of the numbers of people involved on just one Caribbean plantation. Note the inclusion of livestock on the same inventory.

Northumberland Collections Service ZFE 7

An Inventory of Negroes, Horses, and Cattle on Pickerings Plantation January 1st 1857. Property of Ward Cadogan Esquire.

Men	Men continued	Women continued
Adam	Neddy — 25	Cancey
Benny	Ned Joe	Chitter
Ben Yearwood	Moe	Clarissa 10
Bucco	Peter	Dolly
Cambridge — 5	Prince	Dorah
Charles Jemott	Pollydore — 30	Gracey
Crocus	Parow	Kitty
Cain	Richard Cooper	Kitty Sally 15
Charles Fryday	Robin Thorn	Lucy
Charles Rowe 10	Robin	Lubbah
Daniel	Simon — 35	Leonorah
Dancer	Sam, Boson	Molly Andrew
Deago	Tom Driver	Matty 20
Dick Tom	Tom Toney	Mary
Frank — 15	Tom Harden	Mimbo
George	William — 40	Mary Thorn
Howe	Women.	Mary Cadogan
Isaac	Anciller	Mary Bella 25
Jack	Abigale	Nancy
Jack Marvorick 29	Ammo	Nancy, Old
Jack Lammey	Black Hannah	Phillis
John Bailey	Betty 5	Philley
John	Bess Bishop	Philley, Old 30
Lammey	Bessey	Phillis Sarah

Women continued	Boys continued	Boys continued
Pheobe	Harry Frank	Sam Thorn
Peggy	Jeffy Richard 20	Tipp
Ritter	Jack Mingo	Tom
Sarah Thorn 35	John Sambo	Thomas Henr
Sally	Jack	Tom Goodridg
Sibby	James William	Tom Quaco
Olivan	John Niter 25	Thomas, Coop
Tuttabah	Jack Thorn	William
Vilet 40	Jack Reeves	William Hen
Boys	James	**Girls**
Ajacks	Jack Robin	Anno
Anthoney	John 30	Aggy
Ben	John Adam	Betsey
Ben Thomas	Lisbon	Bella
Cooper, Invalede 5	Lewis	Betsey Ann
Cain	Liverpool	Betty Easter
Castiller	Ned 35	Caroline
Cochrane	Pompey	Celia
Carey	Philip	Dinah
Cudjoe 10	Prince	Dinis
Escot	Robert	Elcey
Frederick	Richard 40	Hagar ~~Frank~~
Frank	Sipia	Johannah
Francis	Stephen	Jane Abel
George, Shepherd 15	Sammy Thorn	Jubbah
George	Sammy Dannel	Mary Dosha
Hannebell	Sipia 45	Mariah
Hector	Sam George	~~Malush~~

An Inventory, Continued.

Girls — Continued

Massey	Nanney	Quashebah
Mary Lucy 20	Nancey	Sarah 28
Mary Hannah	Nanney Weatherhead 25	~ ~ ~ ~ ~ ~
Mary Leacock	Nancy Hester	~ ~ ~ ~ ~ ~

Abstract of Negroes		Abstract of Horses		Abstract of Cattle	
Men	40	Horse ~	1	Bulls	17
Women	40	Mare ~	1	Oxen	27
Boys	55	Total ~	2	Cows	22
Girls	28	~ ~ ~ ~ ~ ~		Bull Calves	13
Total	163	~ ~ ~ ~ ~ ~		Heifer Ditto	10
				Total	89

Increase of Negroes 1816

		No.
	On the Esta this day ~ ~ ~ ~ ~	167
	Vilet deliver'd with a Boy call'd Wm Henry ~	1
	Johannah Deliverd of a Girl call'd Aggy ~	1
	Nancy Deliver'd of a Boy call'd John Adam	1
	Total	170

Decrease of Negroes 1816

	Maniwell Shipped for Runing away ~	1
12	A Boy 8 Mos Old named Robert Henry, died of Dysentary	1
18	Hagar Jane died of atrophy ~ ~ ~	1
23	Quashebah died of Dysentary ~ ~	1
	Molly Pheobe died of apoplexy	1
	a Boy call'd John Bowen died	1
	Eve Died of	1
	Remaining this day ~ ~	163
	Total ~	170

16 The Lord takes pleasure in those who fear ...

In the North East there appears to have been little or no personal antagonism between abolitionists and those who had interests in the slavery business. This might reflect the fact that it was a minority business in the region. Although there was considerable press coverage of rebellions in the colonies they never appear to have been linked with local people, yet we know there was a correspondence between a Newcastle merchant and his Jamaican agent in 1831. Neither does the ongoing benefit following the end of slavery in the empire seem to have occasioned comment.

Unlike abolitionists in Liverpool and Bristol, those in the North East appear to have been ignorant of, or unconcerned by, local people with strong connections to slavery. Middle-class Newcastle was small, socially and geographically, with a multiplicity of small, overlapping associations including dissenting religion, assemblies, musical concerts, the Literary and Philosophical Society, charitable activities and, of course, the anti-slavery movement. There were no known slave traders, slave ships or shackled slaves in town to trouble the conscience. All the chains were hidden.

John Graham Clarke's sons; his friend Joseph Lamb, the Newcastle coal merchant and part owner of the glassworks; and his nephew Thomas Clarke all owned plantations in Jamaica run by agents.[124] After Leonard Parkinson and his partner John Graham Clarke both died in 1818, John Altham Graham Clarke appears to have acquired Kinnersley Castle from his father-in-law. He challenged his own father's will on the grounds that he had been incapable of making a considered judgment due to ill health. His younger brother, James, defended the will's integrity, but the case went to Chancery. A number of witnesses were listed to appear, including the widowed Arabella Graham Clarke. Most of those who testified insisted that, although John Graham Clarke had been much diminished by strokes, they were sure that he had been capable of conducting business. James Losh, his close neighbour for over 30 years, insisted that during his last discussion with his friend in December 1816 he had been *compos mentis*. John Altham's case was not upheld.

James Graham Clarke worked at the Newcastle counting house as a glorified chief clerk, handling day-to-day business, including the glass works and relations with tenants on the Fenton Estate. He and John went in hot pursuit of debts and were extremely severe with rent delinquents. They may have extended their business to include others who had married into the family. The ships their father had owned or part-owned are mentioned in business Letter Books in 1818 and again in 1829. Three of John Graham Clarke senior's four remaining daughters had married. The youngest daughter married Robert Hedley, the son of a Newcastle Mayor and coal merchant. Her brother James loaned another sister's husband, the Irish protestant gentleman Richard Butler, £1,500 in 1819, but he caused bad feeling by failing to repay it.

In 1806 the trustees (including Leonard Parkinson) of the six mulatto Peters (Barrett) children, who had been sent to live with John Graham Clarke in 1792, denied Thomas Peters his rights of inheritance. Peters, then living in London, pursued the matter through the courts into the 1820s. The complainant was his guardian, John Graham Clarke, and the judge making the order was Lord Eldon, who was Graham Clarke's relation by marriage. In 1818 John Altham Graham Clarke was drawn into the controversy and was strongly unsympathetic to Thomas Peters' case, presumably because he had a financial interest in the outcome. In 1806 Thomas's younger brother, Samuel, was committed to the Newcastle 'House of Lunacy' for reasons unknown. Samuel Peters was still in the asylum in 1851.[125]

In 1807, after Joseph Graham had died intestate on his Jamaican estate, his uncle, Jacob Graham, removed slaves worth £1,780 to his own Lapland estate and refused to pay for them. Allegedly he was settling his nephew's debts. John Graham Clarke senior later offered Mary Woodcock, Joseph Graham's daughter, £100 for the slaves but she declined and pursued the case. After 1818 her main adversaries were John and James Graham Clarke. James was now listed in trade directories as a 'West India Merchant' and was preoccupied with business and with several legal disputes flowing from family wills, which included much Jamaican business. He never married. In 1827, when he was over 40, Nathaniel Clayton, the family lawyer wrote: 'I'd always thought you a member of bachelor society. Should I be pleased the state of pleasing oneself should continue?' In 1829 both parties and the courts conducted Woodcock's case without referring to the human property

involved and against the background of rising moral repugnance to the institution of slavery. Judgement was given against the brothers.

Close business associates, like the leading abolitionist James Losh, must surely have made their feelings known to the Graham Clarke brothers. When Losh presided over a dinner to celebrate William Turner's 50th year of activity in the town, James Graham Clarke and Joseph Lamb were among the organisers.[126] Earlier, when called as a witness to John Graham Clarke's fitness to

This abolitionist jug was made in Sunderland about 1820.

conduct business, Losh refers to him as 'my friend' and neighbour of 25 years.[127] Losh would also be familiar with the brothers' business partner Joseph Lamb, a joint owner of the Northumberland Glass works but he may not have known he was a slave-owner, and that another business associate, William Plummer, probably shared Jamaican interests. It is reasonable to assume that there was some public knowledge of this family's interest in slaves. It would appear that gentlemen, even those with strong abolitionist convictions, were quite capable of accommodating these contractions in their personal dealings.

The Graham Clarkes' involvement with glass, coal, linen and land in North East England was no doubt much more visible than their plantations in Jamaica in the early 1830s, but it could not have escaped local people's attention that six mulattos had lived with the family for decades and that the family owned a sugar warehouse. William Turner's friend and fellow Unitarian, Robert Rankin, also owned a sugar house in Broad Chare, just off the Quayside. His granddaughter, Harriet Martineau, was living as a semi-invalid in Tynemouth. She was voluble on the slavery issue in print and was to become very prominent in anti-slavery politics on both sides of the Atlantic.

In 1831 James's Jamaican factor and lawyer, John Whittingham, wrote to his employer about the arrangements for transporting goods like sugar and mahogany. He laced his letter with news of the slave rebellion. In spite of that, in June, Whittingham asked James if he intended purchasing Richmond Hill, one of the Barrett estates, together with its slaves. On April 3, 1832 Whittingham wrote to James Graham Clarke:

> you will have heard of the immense destruction of property in St James' most of all the Estates say [sic]works and houses burnt to the ground by Rebellious Negroes set on by those hypocritical preachers Baptists, all the most flourishing part of St James' as to works are gone many I do think will never again be settled. Lapland being mostly wood buildings can not be attempted to become a sugar estate in times like the present … I have therefore desired the Overseer to go on preparing for pasture … the Negroes have now come into [back to?] that property but I fear we have not done with the business. In St Mary's and Vere there appears to have been some commotion … I look on the map as nearly 15 miles square and there is not a building left standing … our situation is deplorable.

By July 10 Whittingham saw order returning. *The Kingston* would be leaving with '11 logs of mahogany, fifteen round logs of Yacco [sic] wood, ninety-six lance woodspars'. He apologised for not having written more often about 'the late ruinous Rebellion' but:

> we don't yet know how it will all end. You have lost no people on Lapland. Sam Graham, a fine young man, a cooper who came home in April, and Morris also a young man learning to be a blacksmith only came home on the sixth of this month are both in jail for charges preferred against them for burning the works of Lapland and Chester Castle … I will inform you of the result' of their trial.

But business went on regardless: 'I have sold Mr Carr Walker [of Morpeth] for Bamboo £620 of working stock'. He promised to send a list of necessary supplies.

By August things seemed calmer, and Whittingham was sending sugar, though 'the prices are miserable.' 'I am happy to say you have lost none of your slaves yet one (Sam) is in jail for trial and is thought will be hung, all the others are behaving themselves at present, we have a continuance of fine reasons [sic] for establishing grass.' Whittingham believed the militia would be needed for some time in case of further revolts, but he was confident enough to plant three acres of ginger. The debates on abolition in Parliament, the new arrangements in Jamaica, the appointment of officials to supervise

CONCENTRATED ESSENCE OF JAMAICA GINGER,
A certain Cure and Preventive of all Nervous Complaints, Spasms, Gout, Rheumatism, &c.

THIS Essence proved, in numerous cases during the prevailing Epidemic of 1832, to be decidedly successful in cases of Cholera, or spasms of the Stomach and Bowels. All the objections that have hitherto attended the administration of Ginger in Powder—such as excessive heat and irritation of the fauces in the act of swallowing, and a subsequent uneasy sensation in the stomach and bowels, &c.—are now completely overcome by the introduction of this elegant preparation, which is made from the pith of the finest Jamaica Ginger that is imported. This pith (one ounce of which is equal in strength to four ounces of powdered Jamaica Ginger) undergoes a tedious chemical process, by which alone the whole of its active principles can be separated; and is now offered to the Public in the very desirable form of a Concentrated Fluid Essence.

The benefits of Jamaica Ginger are advertised in
Newcastle Courant, December 1836.

them and the alleged treachery of members of their own class also filtered into this business correspondence. It is also worth remarking on the likelihood of poor Sam (Graham) being a blood relative.

John Graham Clarke (junior) had spent a lot of time in the 1820s and early 1830s challenging legal decisions and asking the family estate's trustees for financial advances. By the mid-1830s he was experiencing financial difficulties, though he still had his agricultural rents. His brother James sold Fenham Hall in the late 1820s and the house in Pilgrim Street, Newcastle in the early 1830s and moved to Benwell Lodge on the Benwell Estate. He took part in charitable activities and horticultural competitions. In 1836-7 the brothers put in separate claims for compensation under the Act. John claimed with his wife and James with Joseph Lamb, who was at that time Mayor of Newcastle. Their claims listed five other plantation owners with the name of Graham and three with the name of Clarke in St James's parish and the three adjoining parishes in Jamaica, plus another Clarke in a different part of the island. They claimed compensation for freeing 600 slaves and contested the assessment of £18,018. Mary Woodcock claimed £1,708 with interest against the brothers and the arbitration court ruled in her favour, though it is not known if the brothers paid up. During 1837 the receivers paid a visit to John's Frocester estate.

It is also important to note that whilst the Compensation Order and total amount were public knowledge at the time this was not true of the details of the individual claims and the amounts received.

Pilgrim Street in 1834. James Graham Clarke sold the Pilgrim Street house and brewery in the early 1830s.

In 1839 Joseph Lamb subscribed to the retirement appeal for the leading abolitionist, William Turner. It is an interesting fact that Lamb had attended Turner's Unitarian school, as a child in the mid-1780s.

In the 1840s the price of sugar on the world market went into decline and many former slave-owning families' incomes were seriously damaged. This may have happened to the Graham Clarkes. John Altham Graham Clarke died in 1853. His Fenton estate was offered for sale in 1854, and its inventory showed an annual profit of over £3,380. He also owned property at Sutton in East Yorkshire. By 1855 James had sold up his Newcastle holdings and retired to France, where he died in 1857. John's son, another John Altham, born in 1814, appeared to prosper and one branch of the family went off to New Zealand.

Arabella Graham Clarke carried a considerable dowry, because in 1818 her father left each of the four sisters £7,000, plus a share of assets. In 1821 her mother left her another large sum, including South Sea consols at 5 per cent. She never married. She may have shared the fate of many unmarried middle-class daughters, condemned to flit around a family giving emotional support in times of crisis. We know she played this role at times for her famous niece, Elizabeth Barrett-Browning. She spent her first 40 years in her parents' homes in Pilgrim Street, Kenton Lodge and Fenham Hall, then lived with her younger brother James at Benwell Lodge. In 1831 she donated £1 to a Newcastle soup kitchen. By 1840 she had moved to live with her elder brother John at Frocester and Kinnersley Castle, at least until he died in 1853. When she died, at Cheltenham Spa in 1873, she left a small fortune, including over 50 pearl necklaces, plus opals, pearls, diamonds, encrusted brooches, tiaras and gold and silver rings, a 'consolidated fund' and North Eastern Railway stock. She lies in a corner of Frocester Churchyard. The inscription on her grave reads, 'The lord takes pleasure in those who fear him in those that hope in his mercy'.[128] The Graham Clarke family were still ensconced in Kinnersley and Frocester until after 1945.

After Emancipation the Graham Clarkes, no doubt like the majority of those with West Indian interests, sat back and received the financial benefits as long as they were available. There was a more active minority however, like Matthew Forster who, in 1841, was elected MP for Berwick on Tweed, a town with a surprising number of past members and officials with strong connections to the slavery business. These included Wilmot Vaughan, a former Governor of the Leeward Islands and Banestre Tarleton, the 'butcher of Carolina,'[129] whose family were Liverpool slave traders and fierce opponents of abolition. Then there was John Gladstone, the Liverpool slave trader who was nudged out as MP by constituents in 1826.

Forster's family were local to Berwick though he had spent his life as a London merchant in West African trade. It seems that with slavery in the Empire outlawed in 1833-38, a seat in the Commons was an important part of maintaining influence for both the 'legitimate' West Africa trade and helping to cover up dubious dealings involving the illegal slave trade which continued to service Brazil, Cuba and even the southern states of the USA. He was strongly opposed to the continued deployment of the Royal Navy in attempts to suppress this illegal trade. On entering the House he joined a Select Committee on West Africa, becoming a fierce interrogator of witnesses bringing evidence of ongoing connections with slave trading. He survived as an MP until 1853 when he was effectively de-selected for repeatedly buying votes in the Berwick Constituency.[130]

III

Endgame

During the 1860s links to the colonial economy were still maintained, but the details are elusive. Slavery still existed in several parts of the world but its continuation in the heart of democracy, the United States, was very hard to bear. When the opportunity for resistance finally arose the abolitionists were ready. The United States were a long way off and opposition to slavery there was uncomplicated for British abolitionists, if not necessarily for politicians and businessman. Rebellion in the colonies raised different issues. An insurrection of black people in Jamaica in 1865 caused concern, not because of the poor conditions that had prompted the rebellion in the first place, but because of the excessively violent methods sanctioned by the authorities in restoring order. The plight of free black people was of little concern compared to the need to protect 'civilised' society and the empire in a period of growing international competition.

THE INSURRECTION IN JAMAICA.

HORRIBLE ATROCITIES.

Details as to the insurrection in Jamaica, although still of a meagre character, convey a fearful picture of the incidents of the outbreak.

17 A friend and a brother …

After a gap of more than a decade anti-slavery activists in the North East responded to issues raised by the American Civil War. It was a newspaper-led campaign which made the North East one of the key areas of support for the Union side in the war. This activity was followed by an outraged response to the actions of the local and colonial authorities in the face of rebellion in Jamaica. However this was to be a short-lived concern.

In October 1862 a young journalist, Wemys Reid, heard W.E. Gladstone, Chancellor of the Exchequer, address a banquet at Newcastle Town Hall

> … He made one of the notable mistakes of his great career. The Civil War in America, to which Lord Russell had alluded twelve months before, (also at Newcastle) was still raging. I need hardly say that the sympathies of the upper classes were enthusiastically with the South. The names of the public men of eminence who favoured the North might have been counted upon one's fingers. Mr. Gladstone believed in the cause of the Confederates, and in this speech at Newcastle he declared that Jefferson Davis had created not merely an army and a navy, but a nation.[131]

This is no surprise since the Gladstone family fortune derived directly from the slave trade. However the speech was significant for until then the issue of slavery had not been the focus of British interest in the American Civil War. The Confederate South had succeeded in presenting itself as the wounded party, bullied by an imperial Northern regime.

Only a few radicals took the Union side. Among them was Joseph Cowen who had supported the anti-slavery cause since his student days in Edinburgh in the mid-1840s. Cowen was the dominant political figure in Newcastle in second half of the 19th century. He was a very wealthy man. In 1859 he acquired the *Newcastle Chronicle*. He hired first-rate journalists like Richard Reed and W.E. Adams and promoted his great causes through daily and weekly editions. After Gladstone's speech the Civil War became a central issue with strong anti-slavery editorials, regular reports from America and support for the revived anti-slavery campaign in Britain. It could be said that the *Chronicle* was the leading pro-Union provincial paper with an influence which carried far beyond the Newcastle area.[132]

On January 1, 1863, President Lincoln signed the Emancipation Proclamation. A huge celebratory meeting was held at the Nelson Street Music Hall with crowds spilling into the street. This may have been the first meeting of the new campaign anywhere in Britain. Anti-slavery sentiment, so powerful in the 1830s, had been kept alive for a generation by tiny numbers of convinced non-conformists. In the hands of Cowen and Adams it

Newcastle Libraries (local portraits)

Joseph Cowen, Newcastle radical and newspaper owner.

became a mass movement again. It also had a different character. The post-French Revolution abolitionists were deeply paternalistic in rhetoric, always anxious to avoid association with the tocsins of the revolution: liberty, equality, fraternity. The new movement was much less constrained. In 1863 Adams published, for the Emancipation Society, a pamphlet, *The Slaveholders' War: an argument for the North and the Negro*, in which he explained that slave holding was dangerous to white as well as black workers. A victory for the South could mean the spread of slavery, or at least continued unfair competition in the labour market. This was an appeal to class sentiments. Equality between workers of all colours was a central part of campaign propaganda. The war in America had a disastrous impact on workers in the cotton industry in North West England. Supporters of the Confederacy blamed Lincoln and the Union for destitution in England but despite the well-financed attempts of the Confederate lobby to gain support among working people, the cotton workers, who were especially affected by the war, supported the Union.

Cowen's campaign on racial equality had a further propaganda success in the summer of 1863. The British Association for the Advancement of

Science met in Newcastle. Two supporters of the Confederacy, Dr Hunt and Carter Blake, both ethnographers, attended to promote the idea of the racial inferiority of the black person as a justification for the institution of slavery. However Cowen arranged for 'William', an American who had escaped from slavery, to attend the conference. Craft countered the racist arguments with what was reported as good humoured eloquence to the detriment of the gentlemen scientists. *The Chronicle* carried detailed reports (probably by Cowen) of the debate: 'I advise him the next time he comes with his "insulting airs" not to try it on in Newcastle, where a Negro is treated as a friend and a brother.'

The propaganda of the Cowen papers was very important, for it was not true that the area was uniformly pro-Union. Gladstone's speech in Newcastle had been well received when it was made and he was to remain a very popular figure in the region. One of Cowen's tactics was to continue the practice of inviting black abolitionists to the area, organising meetings for them, and following up with full reports in the press suggesting that such events were perfectly normal. It was an effective enough tactic but local support for the Union was only crystallised by the assassination of Lincoln and military success in the war.

The last big issue to motivate the local anti-slavery movement came in autumn 1865. On the November 14, the *Newcastle Daily Chronicle* carried a report headed 'The Insurrection in Jamaica.' The *Newcastle Courant*, a weekly publication, first covered the story three days later. The initial response of both papers was to report terrible violence by the black people. The *Courant*'s story was much more lurid claiming, 'that horrid barbarities and butcheries had been perpetrated … An indiscriminate slaughter of whites seems to have been undertaken.' There was much worse to come. Apparently the Custos (Chief Magistrate of the Parish) had been killed, 'his skull being cleft, and his brains drunk, mixed with rum, by his murderers. However, on November 15 the *Chronicle* carried a long editorial calling on readers to 'suspend judgement until all facts of the events are revealed.' The thoughtful article tried to attribute the likely causes of the rising to the social conditions of the post-slavery peasants and the intense labour discipline of cat and treadmill practiced by the planters. The Newcastle Courant largely repeated the 'official' reports which attributed the behaviour of the black people to primitive impulses unleashed by too much freedom! The issue, and the contrasting responses, burned in the press for about two months.

Gradually the true story behind the insurrection began to filter into the press. In mid-October a Baptist preacher, Paul Bogle, led a group of black men and women peasants into the town of Morant Bay on the south east coast of the island. Thirty years after emancipation there was still awful poverty, severe exploitation and a

Newcastle Daily Chronicle.

WEDNESDAY, NOVEMBER 15, 1865.

THE INSURRECTION IN JAMAICA.

For those who are in want of an argument for slavery based on what is called the barbarous character of the negro, the insurrection in Jamaica is a fortunate event. It is the very thing that was wanted to complete the justification of the maxim, "that man can hold property in man." The outrages that have been committed at Morant Bay have been coloured at all events to suit the purposes of the old slave party. Without inquiring into the cause of this calamity, without waiting for full details of the disturbances, the conduct of the insurgents, even the insurrection itself, has been ascribed to the love of the negro for bloodshed and rapine. Although nothing whatever is yet known of the circumstances that immediately led to the outbreak at Morant Bay, the people who have never scrupled to apologise for slavery have jumped to the conclusion that the disturbances were entirely unprovoked. For our part, we have only to

harsh criminal justice system. The rebels hoped to challenge the planters whom they saw as responsible for their plight. A skirmish took place and the hastily assembled militia opened fire, killing seven peasants. The militia was overwhelmed and the rebels took control of the town. Eighteen people were killed, largely white officials and planters.

The rebels tried unsuccessfully to rally support from other parts of the island. The Governor, Edwin Eyre, marshalled regular troops to suppress the rebellion. The repression cost almost 800 lives, including 350 people executed by instant trials and judicial lynching. Bogle was executed with his brothers and so was George William Gordon, a maroon planter and opposition politician. Over 4500 men and women were flogged with the cat entwined with wire, receiving up to 100 strokes each. As the *Chronicle* pointed out in an editorial headed, 'How Englishmen Suppress a Rebellion' the evidence of the horrors of the massacre was provided by the very army officers and officials who carried it out and were proud of their mission.

The violence was widely reported in the Jamaican press. One example will suffice:

> About 30 were in turn lashed to a gun and catted receiving 50 lashes on the bare back man of war fashion, and the rest committed as rebels. Among the rebels was George Marshal, a brown man of about 25, who, on receiving 47 lashes, ground his teeth and gave a ferocious look of defiance at the Provost Marshall. He was immediately ordered to be taken from the gun and hanged. No time was lost and he was accordingly strung up in the presence of the insurrectionists.

The issue infuriated many people in North East England. Large meetings took place at Clarence Street Methodist Chapel, at West Clayton Street Chapel, at Bewick Street Chapel and in Sunderland, North and South Shields, and Darlington. Protest meetings took place in each of these towns. At Newcastle there were addresses by several ministers of religion who had already spoken at meetings in their own chapels. Whilst most were keen to dismiss the charge that the Jamaican rebels were organised by a Baptist minister, they were enraged by the behaviour of the Jamaican authorities. Joseph Cowen was central to the protest, both through deft use of his newspapers and his willingness to stand on the platform to denounce the Jamaican officials and army officers and those in Britain ready to defend them or cover up for them. Each of the meetings ended with the demand for the recall of Edwin Eyre to face an enquiry and, some argued, to answer a charge of murder in the case of George Gordon. Eyre was recalled, the enquiry took place, but he was found not guilty of the charges.

The anger surrounding the massacre in Jamaica was soon to dissipate. From the start of the movement for abolition in the 1780s the concepts of slave and slavery, were seen as distinct from the sufferings of 'free' labourers in the factories and mines at home. Slavery aroused moral indignation around which people of all classes and religious persuasions could unite. For most, the American Civil War was part of the same issue, even though the prosperity of many parts of the United Kingdom relied on cotton imported from the slave states.

However, the Jamaican peasants were technically free labourers, who (it was generally believed) should be grateful for their emancipation from slavery. Most people believed that the foundation of civilised society was

Courtesy of the Fenwick family Northumberland Collections Service ZFE-61-02 [NRO 7430]

This photograph from the Pickerings estate in Barbados (see page 136) dates from around 1910 but the image could have been from 100 years earlier. The women are carrying sugar cane bundles, and by this time were of course no longer slaves but employees of the Fenwicks.

order and that rebellion should be put down. Besides which, there was the serious question of where post-slavery rebellion might lead. A challenge to 'civilised society' was a challenge to colonial society and its hierarchy and therefore to the very basis on which the Empire existed. There were very few voices in mid-Victorian England who did not share this view, including the middle-class constituency (Joseph Cowen among them), from which the anti-slavery movement's leadership had been drawn. This meant that attention was not focussed on the conditions in Jamaica which had brought about the rebellion but on the unnecessarily harsh punishments meted out to participants and the unseemly pleasure that the soldiers and administrators took in this vindictive work.

As the Governor Eyre enquiry faded from the news, interest in the internal problems of colonial society also diminished. The struggle in the Empire was submerged in the struggle for the Empire, the great obsession which carried on right down to the Great War.

It was to be nearly three quarters of a century before the shadow of plantation society was shaken off in Jamaica. In 1938 a revolt against the labour practices of the giant sugar company, Tate and Lyle, cost the deaths of half a dozen workers. The protest campaign was conducted by Jamaicans who created political parties which led the movement to independence. As war clouds gathered over Europe, these events passed with very little notice in the North East of England.

Afterword – Shining a light on slavery, abolition and North East England

Some members of British society lived lives of considerable luxury on the proceeds of slave labour in the Caribbean and North America. Several people with connections to the North East of England have turned up in this account, for instance the Steads, Trevelyans, Cadogans, Hodgsons, Bennetts, Pinckneys, Halls and Crowleys. As more family papers and public records are examined, others may be found. It is not difficult to understand why the North East has been largely absent from the vast literature on slavery and the histories of region. The region's east-facing ports have their backs to the Atlantic. The North Sea and the Baltic provided more obvious highways for trade and commerce. But the colonies promised substantial wealth, especially for those who were already wealthy, since the investment of surplus resources could quickly bring enormous profits. The source of production was remote, and attendance there was optional, since good agents would do a perfectly good job. Country houses were built, extended or modernised and furnished lavishly. It is quite difficult to trace the exact relationship between this expenditure and the profits of slavery, because few detailed business accounts survive, but John Graham Clarke's building of Kenton Lodge in the late 1780s and the acquisition of Coxhoe, Fenham Hall and the Frocester Estate are clearly attributable to the family's Caribbean wealth. This must surely also be true of John Dobson's restoration of Brinkburn Priory for the Cadogans.

For centuries coal mining and the coal trade occupied centre stage in the North East and created great fortunes for a few people from the back-breaking labour of the many. The region's pre-eminence in the coal trade from the 16th to the 20th centuries meant that its leading businessmen were in regular contact with the London business community and officers of the state. They were an integral part of the national business elite, well placed to take advantage of opportunities on offer. The Carr, Ellison, Cotesworth, Crowley, Ridley, Bowes and Blackett families had members who exploited the possibilities in different ways. Army and Navy officers were also well placed to benefit as the tentacles of empire spread across the globe.

Fenwicks, Ogles, Middletons, Ords and Colvilles all served in the armed forces and subsequently settled into plantation life.

The slave colonies were a productive outlet for young men of ambition and limited means, and the shortage of white men willing to undertake such work meant rapid advance for those who did. Jacob Graham's journey from clerk or overseer to planter is a case in point. Ordinary seamen like Richardson and Robinson also connected to the slave trade by being merchant seaman on Caribbean and North American runs or on retirement from active service as purveyors of marine supplies on both sides of the Atlantic.

The changing habits of consumers also played a part. The national addiction for sugar spread to most social classes from the beginning of the 18th century and had reached the poorest by the 1820s. Sugar was imported directly into the Tyne and three large sugar houses were erected on the riverside in the second half of the 18th century. There was another at Stockton on Tees. Grocers' shops selling sugar, tea, coffee and cocoa proliferated in the region's towns and villages.

It is impossible to quantify the wealth made from colonial slavery and its relationship with the economic and industrial development of Britain, but the sums were clearly enormous. Within a decade of his arrival in Newcastle, John Graham Clarke was cited as a guarantor of the solvency of an important local bank. He must have used this bank for his own cash and so it was available as capital to loan to the region's entrepreneurs. His son, James, invested in the proposed Newcastle to Carlisle canal in the 1820s and his sister, Arabella, had shares in the North Eastern Railway. Though risky, the returns on investment in the industrial revolution were so good that it would be surprising if more sugar money did not find its way into railway development.

In every area of Britain there were families that accumulated gargantuan fortunes from the violent exploitation of slaves. When slavery came to an

Opposite: Newcastle in the 1860s in a lithograph drawn to demonstrate the growth of the town. Much of its prosperity was due to its industrial prowess, and to the coal trade. However, the wealth that was the result of colonial slavery, and the capital thus available for investment, should not be underestimated.

end their bank balances barely suffered, since wise investment elsewhere had secured future incomes. Some slave-owners' extravagance caused personal crises, but compensation for freeing slaves, combined with selling some land, could save a family fortune. John Altham Graham Clarke may be a case in point.

Of those slave owners with North East connections, the Barretts, the Trevelyans and the Cadogan/Fenwicks maintained their Caribbean interests beyond the 1840s. Even if these connections were known, a generation was enough to erase the origins of their wealth from the public mind. Many families slipped into the comfortable obscurity of upper-middle-class English life, attending public schools and Oxford and Cambridge, serving in the armed forces or the Anglican Church, and marrying into families of similar backgrounds. Some of the Trevelyans were prominent public servants but their recent ownership of slaves also seems to have passed without note.

There is an interesting story still to be told of those who made the journey to the American mainland colonies. From the little we know of them we can presume that a significant number became part of the United States political, social and business elite.

The history of abolition in the region, though obviously an honourable activity, has suffered from amnesia too. Historians of the area have virtually ignored it. Perhaps the invisibility of colonial slavery also rendered abolitionists invisible, but there is no good reason why it should have done. It may be that the North Eastern anti-slavery movements were ignorant of the slavery interest in their midst and no local MPs openly supported the West India interest. The North Eastern abolitionists' campaigns were directed at agents in faraway Bristol, Liverpool, London and Jamaica, so it

Opposite: a satirical leaflet from the 1830s, the meaning of which is not immediately clear. It shows us evidence of the way in which the slavery issue had entered common parlance. Long Ridge is Michael Longridge, a prominent abolitionist and proprietor of Bedlington Ironworks. He is accused of hypocrisy in his enthusiasm for the anti-slavery cause while deserting local social reformers (Longridge supported Matthew Bell, an anti-reform MP). The suggestion that the ironworks makes chains and shackles is probably scurrilous, and most likely implies the metaphorical chains of the working classes.

Tyne & Wear Archives DX17.1.43

TO THE
ENEMIES
OF
SLAVERY.

TAKE NOTICE,

THAT there was recently discovered in a Field in the Neighbourhood of Bedlington, at the Top of a LONG-RIDGE, a new Species of crop-ear'd Rat of a Genus unknown to the modern Naturalists;—its particular Habits having been closely observed, we are enabled to give the following Account of one or two of its Peculiarities. On noticing a poor Negro Slave, it has exhibited strong Symptoms of Gratification, and has been seen frisking about with Rats of much meaner Breeding on such Occasions; but when the Clank of the Slave's Chain was heard, or the Rattling of his Iron Collar or Manacles, the Animal seemed entirely to surpass all the known Energies of the Rat Tribe.

From its having been discovered near the Iron Works, it is presumed that it gets its Nourishment from Iron, and it has even been seen casting a complacent Eye on Chains and Shackles in these Works.

It has lately been seen gnawing a Collar that it wore with the Inscription of *Reform* on it; but it now wears a *blue* Collar, and has a large *Bell* at its Side.

The Intention of this Caution is, that Gentlemen should avoid its very ravenous Propensities, as it will even attack and fly ATT WOOD.

is remarkable how big the movement became. Several petitions were signed by hundreds and sometimes thousands. Meetings were very large, often numbering several hundred. This speaks of a strong core of organised and determined activists. After London, which was always the centre of activity, the North East did very well as compared with Manchester, Edinburgh and Glasgow. The region's anti-slavery movement is notable for the number and volubility of female campaigners at a time when women's public activity was frowned upon. Above all, the indefatigable William Turner was a great strength. So was the continuity of campaign personnel in the four main periods – 1791-2, 1814, 1824 and the 1830s. It would be impossible to overestimate the importance of dissenting religion. Quakerism and Unitarianism supplied much of the intellectual and organisational skills, while Presbyterianism and Methodism provided the mass of foot soldiers. Evangelical Anglicanism was probably a small element, but perhaps those of an abolitionist bent made the transition to Methodism.

Newcastle had a strong tradition of political radicalism going back at least as far as the 1760s. This strain was anti-authoritarian almost by instinct. It was there among the seamen and pitmen during the French wars, in the aftermath of Peterloo in 1819, throughout the 1830s and at the birth of Chartism. Tens of thousands could be called out to demonstrations. Anti-slavery sentiment was often displayed with reference to the status of white working people, and such rhetoric was shared with the movement for abolition of slavery.

What of the slaves themselves? Some wealthy households in the North East had black domestic slaves. One is depicted in Thomas Bardwell's 1740 portrait of Captain Robert Fenwick and family at Norham Castle (see page 6). Investigation of churchyards and parish registers has so far yielded half a dozen examples of black people likely to have been slaves, at least originally. After the Mansfield judgment in 1772 it was no longer legal to own a slave in England, and black people in the North East were almost certainly former slaves taking refuge, campaigning or working. For example, Mary Mackham (Macham) escaped from slavery in Virginia, settled in North Shields with a Quaker family and married a local rope maker. She died in 1893.[133] We know only a little of the fate of the six mulatto children of George Goodin Barrett. It is a story worth pursuing as are many of the loose ends left to tie up by future researchers of this long and complex story.

From the end of the 16th century onwards North East England was part of an empire. Like every other area of Britain, it supplied men, women, ideas, money, weapons, ships and commodities to conquer, settle, develop and expand Britain's authority across the globe. The slavery system, with its capacity to produce fabulous wealth, was a key driving force. The chains of slavery may have been largely hidden from sight in the North East, but they were still there, and they were linked to the chains everywhere else. The belief, held by many, that North East England was free from the taint of involvement in the appalling system that was slavery is without foundation. What is true is that once the evil of slavery was properly understood in the North East, men and women in the region became leading advocates of its abolition.

Mary Ann Macham, an escaped slave from Virginia who settled in North Shields.

P. Spence, 'Robert and Mary Spence of North Shields', 1939.

A timeline guide to Atlantic slavery and its abolition

(Entries referring to North East England highlighted)

1501-1600

1502 The first enslaved Africans were taken to the Americas.

1564-1569 Sir John Hawkins, the first English slave trader, took a total of 1,200 Africans to supply the needs of Spanish settlers in Hispaniola (Cuba).

1601-1700

1607 The first permanent English settlement in North America, the colony of Virginia, was founded. It soon became hungry for African labour.

1625 Barbados became an English colony.

1655 England captured Jamaica from Spain.

1672 Charles II formed the Royal African Company to regulate the English slave trade. The company's monopoly ended in 1698.

1701-1800

1702-1713 War of the Spanish Succession. In 1713 Britain gained the right (asiento) to import slaves to Spanish America, granting the franchise to the South Sea Company.

1705 The Virginia General Assembly declared: 'All Negro, mulatto and Indian slaves … shall be held to be real estate. If any slave resist his master … correcting such slave, and shall happen to be killed in such correction … the master shall be free of all punishment'.

1720 The South Sea Company crashed due to massively inflated share prices (the South Sea Bubble). The company recovered and was the main source of investment in slavery until the end of the trade.

1730-1739 First Maroon War in Jamaica. The first great rebellion in the Caribbean.

1745 Birth of Olaudah Equiano.

1756-63 Seven Years War. Britain gained several Caribbean colonies.

1759 Birth of William Wilberforce.

1760 Slave rebellion in Jamaica.

1760 Birth of Thomas Clarkson.

1760 Birth of William Turner, Newcastle Unitarian minister, abolitionist.

1772 Chief Justice Lord Mansfield ruled that enslaved people in England could not be forced to return to the West Indies (The Somerset Case).

1775-83 American War of Independence. France seized Grenada, Tobago and St Kitts from Britain. After Peace of Versailles, Grenada and St Kitts were returned.

1783 131 Africans were thrown overboard from the slave ship *Zong*. This led to an insurance dispute but not a murder trial. The scandal caused outrage and strengthened the campaign for abolition.

1786 Publication of Thomas Clarkson's *An essay on the slavery and commerce of the human species*.

1787 Founding of The Society for the Abolition of the Slave Trade.

1788 Newcastle Common Council ask Parliament to enquire into the conditions of the slave trade.

1789 Publication of Olaudah Equiano's *The Interesting Narrative of the Life of Olaudah Equiano, or Gustavus Vassa, the African*.

1789 Start of the French Revolution in July. News of its ideas of liberty, equality and fraternity led to discontent in the slave colonies.

1791 Newcastle Abolition Committee founded.

1790 The first abolition bill was presented to the House of Commons by William Wilberforce. It was unsuccessful.

1791-1804 The Haitian Revolution was triggered by a slave uprising in St Domingue in 1791. Toussaint L'Ouverture led an army of ex-slaves to victory. St Domingue changed its name to Haiti and became the first independent black republic in 1804.

1792-1800 Three failed attempts to get abolition through Parliament delayed by War with France.

1794 France abolished slavery. All enslaved people in her colonies freed.

1795-96 The Maroons were defeated in the second Maroon War in Jamaica.

1795 Fédon's Rebellion in Grenada. Enslaved people seized control of large parts of the island. They were defeated by British troops in 1796.

1795 Stanfield's Poem, *The Guinea Voyage* published.

1796 Napoleon seized power in France restoring slavery in its colonies.

1801-1900

1802 First West India dock opened dedicated to receiving goods from the Caribbean.

1802-03 Toussaint L'Ouverture, was taken prisoner by French in 1802. He died in captivity in 1803.

1803-15 Napoleonic Wars. Congress of Vienna confirmed British control of St. Lucia, Tobago and the Guiana colonies.

1807 British parliament abolished the transatlantic slave trade. The US also banned the slave trade from 1808.

1808 The British West Africa Naval Squadron was established in an attempt to suppress illegal slave trading. Between 1810 and 1865 they freed nearly 150,000.

1814 New petitioning campaign launched in Newcastle and other towns in the North East.

1815 The Congress of Vienna. Britain pressured France, the Netherlands, Portugal and Spain to abolish their slave trades.

1816 Bussa's slave rebellion in Barbados was savagely crushed.

1817 Spain agreed to end the Spanish slave trade.

1817 All slave owners were to provide a list of all the enslaved people they owned every two years under the Slave Registration Act.

1818 Death of Newcastle's West India merchant and plantation owner, John Graham Clarke.

1823 British forces brutally suppressed a slave rising in Demerara causing the deaths of 250 enslaved people. Britain outraged when Rev. John Smith of the London Missionary Society received the death sentence for his part.

1823 Formation of the Anti-Slavery Committee in London. They campaigned for total abolition of slavery.

1824 Several new Abolition Committees established across the region.

1831 In Jamaica a major slave revolt called 'The Baptists' War' was led by Baptist preacher Sam Sharpe. It was brutally suppressed.

1831 St Domingue's name changed to Haite.

1831 Nat Turner leads a slave rebellion in Virginia.

1832 The Great Reform Act introduced new MPs with anti-slavery sympathies.

1833 Abolition of Slavery Act passed. Although the Act was scheduled to take effect in the British West Indies in 1834 it declared that the former enslaved people must serve a period of apprenticeship before receiving full emancipation. Compensation of slave holders for the loss of their property caused great anger amongst abolitionists.

1833 William Wilberforce died on 29 July, three days after the Act was passed.

1838 Full emancipation of enslaved people in British territories.

1865 The end of the American Civil War. The Thirteenth Amendment marked the abolition of slavery in the USA.

1865 The Morant Bay rising in Jamaica. 17 Europeans were killed and 32 wounded. The authorities reacted violently declaring martial law. In reprisals 400 blacks were killed.

1886 Slavery abolished in Cuba.

1888 Slavery abolished in Brazil.

Further reading

There are no books which deal specifically with the slavery and abolition question and the North East connection, but the following provide very good portraits of the region's history at relevant points.

Joan Allen, *Joseph Cowen and Popular radicalism on Tyneside 1829-1900* (Monmouth, 2007)

Robert Colls & Bill Lancaster, eds, *Newcastle upon Tyne: A Modern History* (Chichester, 2001)

Norman McCord, *North East England: The Region's Development 1760-1960* (London, 1979)

Nigel Todd, *The Militant Democracy: Joseph Cowen and Victorian Radicalism* (Whitley Bay, 1979)

Kathleen Wilson, *The Sense of the People: Politics, Culture and Imperialism 1715-1785* (Cambridge, 1995)

The literature on slavery is vast. I list a few books which, as well as being very informative, are also a very good read.

Madge Dresser, *Slavery Obscured: The Social History of the Slave Trade in an English Provincial Port* (London 2001)

Laura Fish, *Strange Music* (a novel) (London, 2008)

Adam Hochschild, *Bury the Chains* (London, 2006)

Marcus Rediker, *The Slave Ship* (London 2007)

James Walvin, *The Trader The Owner The Slave* (London, 2007)

James Walvin, *Black Ivory* (London, 2001)

Slavery Today

It would be consoling to think that this story ended with the good news that slavery itself was banished from the globe. Unfortunately this is just not true. It is estimated that today, in 2008, there are more than 12 million enslaved people. Of this number 2.4 million have been trafficked, mainly women and girls for the sex trade. [International Labour Organisation estimate]

Contemporary slavery takes many forms:

•Bonded Labour-people trapped in debt that they have to repay with forced labour.

•Human trafficking-people transported and forced to work against their will.

•Descent-based slavery-people who are born into a group that society discriminates against and treats as property.

•Forced domestic servitude-often hidden and forced to work in private homes.

•Child labour-including prostitution and child soldiers.

For further information visit the web-site of Anti-Slavery International: http://www.antislavery.org

Anti-Slavery International
Thomas Clarkson House
The Stableyard
Broomgrove Road
London
United Kingdom
SW9 9TL
tel: +44 (0)20 7501 8920
fax: +44 (0)20 7738 4110
email: info@antislavery.org
Registered Charity 1049160
Company Limited Guarantee 3079904

Abbreviations and notes

Abbreviations

BL   British Library

DNB   Dictionary of national Biography

DRO   Durham Record Office

GRO/GCP Gloucester Record Office/Graham Clarke Papers

LP   Newcastle Literary and Philosophical Society

NA   National Archives

NC   *Newcastle Courant*

NUSC   Newcastle University Library Special Collections

[CET]   Trevelyan Papers-Charles Edward Trevelyan

NLS   Newcastle City Library Local Studies

NRO   Northumberland Record Office (Northumberland Collections Service)

TWA   Tyne and Wear Archives

1 Stephen Harbottle, The Reverend William Turner: *Dissent and Reform in Georgian Newcastle Upon Tyne* (Newcastle, 1997).

2 Jeffrey Smith, 'James Murray (1732-1782): Radical and Dissenter', *North East History*, Volume 32, 1978, pp 55-79.

3 John Wilkes, the radical MP for Middlesex in the 1760s, was repeatedly elected and barred from the House of Commons for attacking the Government. He enjoyed wide support in the provinces.

4 Thomas Bewick (1753-1828) the Newcastle wood-engraver.

5 Thomas Bewick, *A Memoir of Thomas Bewick*, ed. Montague Weekley pp 59-60.

6 http://gbgm-umc.org/umw/wesley/thoughtsuponslavery.stm

7 Thomas Jackson, ed., *The Works of John Wesley*, (London, 1872), Volume XI, pp 59-79.

8 Geoffrey Milburn, *The Travelling Preacher: John Wesley in the North-East of England 1742-1790*, (The Wesley Historical Society North-East Branch, 2003).

9 Thomas Clarkson, *The History Of The Rise, Progress And Accomplishment Of The Abolition Of The Slave Trade By The British Parliament*, [1807 ed.], (Kessinger Publishing's Rare Reprints, 2007), Chapter XXI, p 218.

10 TWA 589/16/58, p 56, February 9, 1788, and 589/16/59 p 56, Feb 16, 1788.

11 passim, Harbottle.

12 NC, January 7, 21 and February 4, 11, 18, 25, March 17, 24, 31 1792. I am indebted to Ruth Blower for scouring the local press and other sources for evidence of these events and people.

13 Peter Livsey, 'Republic of Letters,' *North East History*, Volume 39, 2008.

14 Thomas Paine (1737-1809), author of *The Rights of Man* (1791 & 1792) was the *bête noire* of conservatives.

15 F. O'Gormon, 'The Paine Burnings of 1792-3,' *Past and Present*, 193, 2006, pp 115-147.

16 William Wilberforce (1759-1833), *DNB* online.

17 *NC*, March 25, 1793.

18 http://www.archive.org/details/guineavoyagepoem00stanuoft

19 Peter van der Merwe, 'James Field Stanfield' *DNB* online.

20 Newcastle Libraries, Local Studies, Tracts: *Abolition of Slavery*, no date, Volume 1.

21 NRO, 3456. Trotter Letters; 'Dr Thomas Trotter', *Dictionary of National Biography* online. In 1802, after finally retiring from the Navy on health grounds, Trotter wrote plays, was active in the Literary & Philosophical Society, studied the problem of 'choke damp' among coal miners and mental disorders, and was a firm opponent of the press gang. He continued to support the abolition of slavery until he died in 1832.

22 E.I. Carlisle (Revised P. Wallis), 'Dr Thomas Winterbottom,' *DNB* online.

23 Olaudah Equiano (1745-1797) was well regarded and the best-known black abolitionist. He visited Newcastle in 1791. See James Walvin, *The Trader The Owner The Slave*, (London 2007), pt 3.

24 A counterweight to Earl Grey, Sir John Scott (1751-1838), son of a Newcastle coal dealer and Lord Chancellor for 27 years as Lord Eldon, was arguably the most reactionary figure in the governing elite.

25 As the 2nd Earl Grey, Charles Grey (1764-1845), the Northumbrian land owner, was the leading advocate of reform among the ruling elites.

26 Neil Sinclair, *Wearside and the Slave Trade*, http://www.bbc.co.uk/wear/content/articles/2007/05/08/abolition_wearside_and_slave_trade_feature.html

27 Wayne Akerson, *The African Institution (1807-1827) and the antislavery movement in Great Britain* (New York, 2005).

28 *NC* December 28, 1813, March 15, May 19, 26, July 13, 1814.

29 Christopher Lloyd, *The Navy and the Slave Trade* (London, 1949).

30 E.P. Thompson, *The Making of the English Working Class* (London, 1963), pp 708-709.

31 *NC* December 2, 1820. Earl Grey was seen locally as a friend to reform.

32 Thomas Fowell Buxton (1786-1845), brewer, reformer and abolitionist from Quaker stock though he was an Anglican. Olwyn Mary Blouet, 'Thomas Fowell Buxton', *DNB* online.

33 Robin Blackburn, *The Overthrow of Colonial Slavery 1776-1848* (London, 1988) pp 421-426.

34 *NC* March 27, May 22, 1824.

35 Emilia Viotti da Costa, *Crowns of Glory, Tears of Blood: The Demerara Slave Rebellion of 1823* (Oxford, 1994).

36 Thomas Wentworth Beaumont (1792-1848), owner of lead mines, was a Tory who moved over to the (mildly) radical cause. In 1826 he quarrelled with Grey and Lambton leading to a duel between himself and Lambton on Bamburgh beach. Though shots were fired neither was injured.

37 NRO, 3948/65, 93 and123.

38 Lit & Phil Library Room Tracts 042/4v 75 no 4. Observations on the Demerara Memorial.

39 Thomas Denman (1779-1854), son of a ship's surgeon, a lawyer who advocated legal reform including the abolition of slavery. He had defended Queen Charlotte and became Lord Chief Justice. Stephen Lushington (1782-1873) a judge, administrator and abolitionist. Two female members of his family made compensation claims with the Trevelyans in 1837. Daniel O'Connell (1775-1847) was the leading Irish politician of the day.

40 Sir George Stephen, *Anti-Slavery Recollections: a series of letters addressed to Mrs Beecher Stowe* (London, 1854), Letter VIII, pp 120-124.

41 TWA DX1100/6; NC August 15, 1830.

42 Edward Pearce, *Reform! The Fight for the 1832 Reform Act* (London, 2004).

43 NRO, SANT/BEQ/28/1/04/96-98, 104-105.

44 William Woodman, a member of the Newcastle Antiquarians, preserved the Morpeth Society's papers.

45 op cit. Blackburn p 455.

46 Report of the Agency Committee of the Anti-Slavery Society (London, 1832: [republished by Cornell University Library Digital Collections, 2006]).

47 op cit., Blackburn pp 432-435, and thereafter.

48 *NC* February 23, March 3, 1832.

49 *NC* August 9, 1833.

50 Clare Midgley, *Women Against Slavery: The British Campaigns 1780-1870* (London, 1992), pp 62-63.

51 Newcastle Ladies' Petition, TWA DX17/1/112.

52 op cit., Midgley, pp 62-63.

53 A Government loan was raised by Nathan Rothschild and Moses Montefiore.

54 The Slavery Abolition Act of 1833 (citation 3 & 4 Will. IV c. 73), summary from Wikipedia online.

55 Sir George Stephen, *Anti-Slavery Recollections: a series of letters addressed to Mrs Beecher Stowe*, London, 1854, Letter VIII, pp 120-124.

56 All quotes from *NC*, August-September, 1833.

57 *NC* December 26, 1835.

58 Ronald M. Gifford, 'George Thompson,' *American National Biography Online*.

59 *NC* April 9, 1836.

60 Referred to in Charles H Wesley, 'The Abolition of Negro Apprenticeship in the British Empire', *The Journal of Negro History*, Vol. 23, No. 2 (Apr., 1938), pp. 155-199.

61 *NC* 21st September 21, 1838.

62 *NC* August 3, 1838.

63 TWA 3744/389, Ladies' Minute Book.

64 *Northern Liberator* (NL), 5 January 1839.

65 op cit., Thompson, *ANBO*.

66 Obit. NC December 23, 1870, Thomas Doubleday (1790-1870), poet, song writer, manufacturer and radical politician.

67 *NC* February 1, 1839.

68 It is not known if local abolitionists were aware of Lamb's West Indian interests. It is quite unlikely that his claim for compensation would be known publicly.

69 op cit., Midgley, pp 122-124.

70 *NC* 1st January, 1847

71 'Elizabeth Pease Nichol' and 'John Pringle Nichol', *DNB* online.

72 O'Donnell, Elizabeth, *There's Death in the Pot! Ethical consumerism and the North East of England in the age of slavery*, unpub. MS, Newcastle, 2007.

73 The Merchant Adventurers Company (Guild) was the association of businessmen who had controlled business and political life since the 13th century.

74 A chaldron was just less than a modern ton in weight.

75 D. Levine & K. Wrightson, *The Making of an Industrial Society: Whickham, 1560-1765* (Oxford, 1991).

76 The second overthrow of the Stuarts which firmly established the Protestant Succession.

77 Shipping lists of arrivals, departures and sometimes cargoes, were published weekly in most Newcastle newspapers in the 18th and 19th centuries.

78 National Archives, ADM 35/4197, The Pay Book of HMS *Newcastle* for September 1816,.

79 William Moraley, *The Infortunate: The Voyage and Adventure of William Moraley an Indentured Servant* (Newcastle, 1743), Susan E Klepp & Billy G Smith, eds, (University of Pennsylvania Press, 1992).

80 R.S. Davies, compiler, *Georgia Pacquet, Captain William Manson's Indentured Servants, September 1775* (Quaker Records in Georgia, n.d.), pp 204-5.

81 Gwenda Morgan & Peter Rushton, *Eighteenth-century criminal transportation: the formation of the criminal Atlantic* (Palgrave, 2004).

82 See Cook Letters in Chapter 14.

83 NRO, Marr letters, SANT/BEQ/28/1/130A-130B-131-140-148A.

84 NRO, Middleton Papers, ZMI/B30/I/14 June 10, 1769.

85 Suffolk Record Office, (Ipswich), Crowley Papers HA1/GD/5/1-17.

86 R. Smith, *Sea Coal for London* (London, 1961), pp 155-62.

87 Ann Lake of Longbenton was the daughter of Robert Lake, Commissary General to the British Army in North America, who acquired enormous landholdings there after the Seven Years War 1757-63.

88 John Sykes, *Local Records* (Newcastle 1828), Volume 1, p 203.

89 D. Eltis, S.D. Behrendat, H.S. Klein & D. Richardson, *Transatlantic Slave Trade Data Base*, (Cambridge, 2002).

90 See Chapter 8 for William Richardson's experience.

91 NRO, Cook letters, ZCK/3/36/25-42.

92 NRO ZCE/10. Ralph Carr's Letter Book: American Letters.

93 Matthew White Ridley had become MP for Newcastle, and was succeeded by his son, also Matthew, in that post. He was also Governor of the Merchant Adventurers Company, a trader in coal and wine, a purchaser of South Sea shares and a major landowner in Northumberland. His soldier brother, John, was killed fighting North American

revolutionaries in the War of Independence.

94 A.W. Purdue, *The Ship That Came Home* (London, 2004), pp 92-96; www.theblacketts.com/gedcom

95 H. Chestnutt, D.R. Hamer, H.P.M. Laurens & G.C. Rogers, eds, *The Papers of Henry Laurens* (Charleston, 2002), Volume 16, pp 202-204.

96 NRO, Stead letters, ZBL 234.

97 NRO, Cook letters, ZCK/3/36/25-42.

98 NRO, ZR1/25/13.

99 L&P, Knott Local D43/9, H.M. Richardson, 'Robert Hutton' *Sunderland Antiquarian Society*, Volume IX, 1908. It is possible the *The Spy* is actually *The Fly.* referred to in the previous chapter (page 102). This may be the result of orthographic confusion.

100 Richardson later wrote a substantial and highly informative autobiography, though it was nearly 100 years before it was published as one of the very rare accounts of an 18th century seaman's life before the mast. William Richardson, *A Mariner of England* (London, 1908 [2005 ed]).

101 ibid. Richardson, pp 27-31,41.

102 Marcus Rediker, *The Slave Ship: A Human History* (New York, 2007).

103 op cit., Richardson, pp 49-50,61,64-5,73,130.

104 Samuel Robinson, *A Sailor Boy's Experience aboard a slave ship* (Wigton, 1867 [1996 ed.]), pp 21-23. Crimps were men employed to inveigle, bribe or bully sailors into registering for voyages.

105 NRO 2360, Henderson letter, March 12 1837.

106 See Valerie Glass, 'An industers man,' *North East History*, Volume 39, 2008.

107 East Riding Archives (Beverley), ERA DDKE/8; ERA, DDGR/42/19/98 Grimston Family papers; Gloucester Record Office, Graham Clarke Papers. (GRO/GCP) The papers are arranged in nine boxes in broad categories e.g. Family, Business, Miscellaneous, etc.

108 C. Petley, '"Legitimacy" and Social Boundaries: Free People of Colour and the Social Order in Jamaican Slave Society,' *Social History*, [2005], Volume 30, Number 4; C. Petley, 'Slavery, Emancipation and the Creole World View of Jamaican Colonists, 1800 - 1834', *Slavery and Abolition*, 2005, Vol 26, Number 1.

109 GRO, Graham Clarke Papers, testimony of James Wilson, clerk.

110 op cit., Purdue pp 92-96, and www.theblacketts.com/gedcom

111 NRO ZBK/C/2/1/1 Christopher Blackett Letter Book.

112 op cit., Purdue 82-83.

113 NRO 2DE/44/7-9, Delaval Papers (Hussey & Manesty).

114 NRO ZRI/53/5 & 6, Tobias Frere in Barbados.

115 Newcastle University Library Special Collections, Trevelyan Papers, CET, August 5, 1770 3 Feb 1768.

116 Mary Sirault, *The Trevelyan Letters to 1840*, Somerset Record Society (Taunton, 1990), p x-xi.

117 TWA House Carpenters Book, GU/HMT4, Letter attached. No number.

118 *NC* September 10, 1833.

119 Newcastle University Library Special Collections, Trevelyan Papers, CET/12/7.

120 Ibid. CET/11/24.

121 Ibid. CET/12/1-3,8.

122 NRO ZFE10. The Fenwicks present a most interesting case of Colonial American involvement. Most of the families seem to have gone to the Southern colonies and, as well-to-do people, were likely to have been slave holders perhaps even including the Quaker Fenwicks. Family and other business connections with other North Eastern migrants, Ogles, Marrs, Johnsons and Pinckneys make this a valuable research project on both sides of the Atlantic.

123 NRO ZFE 61-63.

124 GRO/GCP.

125 Samuel Peters appears on the 1851 Census at the Asylum in Westgate Ward.

126 *NC* December 30, 1831.

127 GRO/GCP

128 GRO/GCP and Photographic Collection of tombstones.

129 Tarleton, a commander of British forces in the American War of Independence, was remembered for his savage treatment of captured American troops.

130 Marika Sherwood, *After Abolition: Britain and the Slave Trade since 1807* (London, 2007) pp 64-78.

131 J. Stuart Reid, (ed.) *The Memoirs of Sir Wemyss Reid, 1842-1885* (London, 1905) chapter 1. (Internet Book).

132 This chapter relies on Nigel Todd, *The Militant Democracy* (Whitley Bay, 1991), and Joan Allen's *Joseph Cowen and Radical Tyneside* (London, 2007).

133 Sean Creighton, 'Black People in the North East of England', *North East History*, 39, 2008.

Acknowledgements

The story of North East involvement in the slavery business is complex, and without the heightened interest aroused in 2007 it may well have remained hidden. A large team of volunteers scrutinised several archive collections and everyone was surprised by the amount of material that came to light. Even so, one of the largest archives in the region, the Durham Record Office, plus those at Teesside Record Office, Cumberland Record Office and the local studies collections at the main public libraries in Newcastle, Sunderland and North and South Shields, have received only limited attention. Productive searches at the Northumberland Record Office, Tyne and Wear Archives, University of Newcastle's Robinson Library Special Collections and the Newcastle Literary & Philosophical Society library suggest that an enormous amount of material awaits recovery elsewhere. This book is a provisional account of the work and leaves many threads loose. Further research is needed.

I also wish to acknowledge those who read early versions of the manuscript and gave me useful pieces of information. Sean Creighton stands out. He put his very considerable knowledge at my disposal and has supported the effort at every stage. Dave Harker and Jonathan Neale read drafts giving much deserved criticism. They followed this up with very helpful suggestions on structure. My good friend Willie Thompson was very helpful throughout. Peter Livsey read it twice and provided very detailed corrections. His own work on the Lit & Phil and that of Valerie Glass, Patricia Hix, Tamsin Lilley, Margaret Woolley, Ann-Marie Nichol, and Liz O'Donnell have been invaluable. Sauda Motara opened a very important door to the involvement of the Graham Clarke family. Ann Creighton also read it very carefully. Hazel Edwards, Sue Wood, Melanie Wood, Kay Easson, Pam Wilson, Keith Gilroy and Carole Scott have been very encouraging. Two undergraduate history students, Ruth Blower of Newcastle University and Rachael McCluskey of Nottingham University, produced excellent detailed research on Newcastle abolitionist activity. I hope they will publish their work.

I am very grateful to Jim Walvin, the doyen of slavery studies in Britain. Jim was my tutor at the University of York many years ago, and willingly, warmly and with his customary good humour, he returned to this role, answering many questions and reading a draft whilst on a research trip in Virginia. As always, Sally Mitchison has offered sharp criticism and affectionate suggestions. Finally, Anna Flowers and Vanessa Histon of Tyne Bridge Publishing have been immensely helpful. They have been tremendous editors, full of excellent suggestions about content, layout and style, supporting the project on a daily basis.

John Charlton, 2008

Index